3 DAYS IN SEPTEMBER

First published in 2004 by Liberties Press
51 Stephens Road | Inchicore | Dublin 8 | Ireland
www.libertiespress.com | info@libertiespress.com
Editorial: +353 (1) 402 0805 | sean@libertiespress.com
Sales and marketing: +353 (1) 453 4363 | peter@libertiespress.com

Trade enquiries to CMD Distribution
55A Spruce Avenue | Stillorgan Industrial Park | Blackrock | County Dublin
Tel: +353 (1) 294 2560
Fax: +353 (1) 294 2564

Copyright the contributors, 2004

ISBN 0-9545335-4-2

2 4 6 8 10 9 7 5 3 1

A CIP record for this title is available from the British Library

Compiled by Peter O'Connell and Seán O'Keeffe
Edited by Seán O'Keeffe
Cover design by Liam Furlong at space.ie
Cover photograph by John Donat

Printed in Ireland by Colour Books
Unit 105 | Baldoyle Industrial Estate | Dublin 13

3 DAYS IN SEPTEMBER

WHEN THE POPE CAME TO IRELAND

LIB
ERT
IES

CONTENTS

5

PUBLISHERS' NOTE

The colour photographs in this book, which originally appeared in *The Phoenix Park Dublin, 29th September 1979: The Pastoral Visit of Pope John Paul II* (Criterion Press), are reproduced by kind permission of John Donat, who sadly passed away as this book was being prepared for the press. The publishers are also grateful to John Donat's son Jasper and to Scott Tallon Walker for allowing the images to be reproduced. All black-and-white photographs are reproduced courtesy of Independent Newspapers Ireland (Liam Mulcahy, Group Photographic Manager). To order a copy of any of these photographs, please contact Independent Photo Sales at 01 804 4333.

The publishers would like to thank all the contributors to this book, and everyone who assisted in its production, including Maeve Binchy, Margaret Egan, Peter Hennelly, Daibhí MacDomhnaill, Mary Maher, Liam Mulcahy, Tom Ryan, Ronnie Tallon and Sue Watters; also friends, partners and relatives whom we have pestered mercilessly in an effort to attract both ideas and contributors.

The piece by Nell McCafferty on page 117 originally appeared in the 17 April 1986 issue of *In Dublin* magazine and was reprinted in *Goodnight Stories: Selected Articles of Nell McCafferty* (1987). The article, copyright Nell McCafferty, is reproduced here by permission of Attic Press Ltd, Crawford Business Park, Crosses Green, Cork, Ireland. The piece by Mark Harkin on page 89 and the one by Kevin Myers on page 159 originally appeared in the October 1999 issue of *AMDG: A Publication of the Irish Jesuits*. They are reprinted here by kind permission of *AMDG*. The extract from the Austin Clarke poem on page 146 is reprinted here by kind permission of R. Dardis Clarke, 17 Oscar Square, Dublin 8.

The publishers sought contributions to this book from people from diverse backgrounds, religious, political and otherwise, and do not aim to promote any particular view of the papal visit of 1979. The contributions reflect a wide range of views on the visit and do not necessarily represent the views of either Liberties Press or the Simon Communities of Ireland.

The publishers would also like to take this opportunity to point out to our more eagle-eyed readers that we are aware that the Pope's visit to Ireland took place on September 29 and 30, and October 1 (i.e. on two days in September and one in October). On reflection, we decided, along with the producers of the documentary *Krakatoa: East of Java* *, not to allow the truth get in the way of a good story – or title. We hope you enjoy the book.

* The island of Krakatoa lies to the *west* of Java.

Introduction

I regret very much that I was not in Ireland for the historic visit of Pope John Paul II in September 1979. It was the first time ever that a Pope had visited our country, which had once so prided itself on being 'the Island of Saints and Scholars' and, indeed, rejoiced in the description of 'Catholic Ireland'. Perhaps no succeeding Pope will ever visit Ireland – or at least not in the lifetime of anyone alive today. The next Pope will have many more pressing priorities, for a Pope is a type of universal monarch, and the Catholic universe of the twenty-first century will be much more focused on Africa, Asia and Latin America than on an off-shore European island.

My reasons for not being in Ireland for those three days in the autumn of 1979 were mostly domestic. We were living in London at the time: my eldest son had only just started primary school, and my younger son was still a babe in arms. I was at that phase of wifehood and motherhood when the responsibilities of the home seem to cause major preoccupation: the life of a working mother is seldom one of personal freedom.

We had, as it happened, spent the month of August 1979 in Ireland, in Connemara and County Clare. A pall of gloom had hung over the country, it seemed to me, after the events of Mullaghmore in County Sligo. On 27 August, Lord Mountbatten and two innocent teenage boys – his fourteen-year-old grandson and a seventeen-year-old boatman – were blown up by the IRA. On the same day, eighteen British soldiers were killed (and eight seriously injured) at Warrenpoint in County Down. These melancholy events were distressing, and I was constantly quarrelling with my brother James in Dublin about the situation in the North. I loved him dearly, but I could not accept his passionate republicanism and Provisional Sinn Féin politics.

I really loathed the turn that the Troubles had taken. These 'soft targets' of innocent teenage boys – soldiers join armies to fight, but civilians do not go out on fishing excursions with the expectation of being annihilated – were, to me, inexcusable. How, I wondered, could members and supporters of the Provisional IRA approach the altar rails and consider themselves in a state of Christian grace? And how could any priest grant absolution, unless he was convinced that 'a firm purpose of amendment' had been avowed – that is, unless the penitent promised not to do it again? I knew many Irish people in England at this time – the broadcaster Henry Kelly was one who shared these moments – who simply felt like walking up and down outside Sinn Féin headquarters with a placard proclaiming: 'NOT IN MY NAME'.

I give this as the political, and even personal, context of the papal visit. My first considerations were, as I say, domestic. I think there might also have been the matter of expense: before the advent of Ryanair, Aer Lingus charged very fancy prices for crossing the Irish Sea – and no newspaper had invited me to comment or report on the papal visit. Perhaps I was vexed about that. But I did feel, also, a sense of alienation about the political situation in Ireland. I had fallen out with several Dublin friends at the time who, I felt, were too quick to excuse what the IRA and 'the republicans' were doing in our name.

So I stayed put, and watched it all on television in London. But from the moment John Paul II entered Irish airspace, I had a rush of all the exile's yearnings, wishing and wanting to be there in those green fields of home. There was a palpable sense of radiance about the whole occasion. The entire country seemed to have turned out to greet him. (It was actually a third of the entire population – which is probably more than had ever been gathered in one spot either before or since.) The roars of approval that greeted John Paul II were the *cead mile fáilte* to end all *cead mile fáilte*s.

When the Holy Father spoke at Drogheda, I knew, immediately, that this was a historic moment. He spoke, it seemed to me, sensitively and yet forcefully, and gave the true Christian message of the Gospel of the Sermon on the Mount.

'Christianity,' he said, 'does not command us to close our eyes to . . . unjust social or international situations. What Christianity does forbid is to seek solutions to these situations by hatred . . . Violence destroys what it claims to defend: the dignity, the life, the freedom of human beings.' Further violence in Ireland, he said, 'will only drag down to ruin the land you claim to love and the values you claim to cherish.'

And then came the peroration which I recognised, at the deepest level of my consciousness, as being so historically significant. 'On my bended knees,' the Holy Father said, 'I beg you to return to the ways of peace. You may claim to seek justice. I, too, believe in justice and seek justice. But violence only delays the days of justice. Violence destroys the work of justice.'

Oh, bravo, and *bravissimo*, I thought, sitting in the chair with my younger son in my arms. It is so important to say this, I thought. It is so important that someone in authority should articulate it, loud and clear. Please, please turn away from blowing up young boys in Sligo boats, and families and children in Belfast restaurants, and tourists shopping at Harrod's, and innocent Irish brothers who had met each other for a drink in Birmingham. We know, we understand, that there are graves injustices to be remedied – serious inequalities, great sources of bitterness, and sometimes a quite dreadful inheritance of discrimination – and wicked acts of violence on all sides. But any Catholic involved in acts of political terrorism has now heard it from the lips of the Supreme Pontiff of the Catholic Church: he was begging the paramilitaries to resist the ways of violence and choose the path of peace.

There is a corny American catchphrase, which raises a sardonic smile this side of the Atlantic: 'What would Jesus do?' But it is altogether plausible that this is precisely the plea that Jesus Christ might have made at Drogheda. I felt, from that moment on, that there would come a day of hope and a day of peace, however imperfect.

*

When Louis XVI of France went to the guillotine in 1793, it was said that a hundred thousand witnesses would tell a hundred thousand stories of that day. The comparison is not perhaps felicitous, but the principle is the same: a hundred thousand people – or indeed one and a quarter million people – will have their own different versions, interpretations and recollections of the papal visit to Ireland in the autumn of 1979. This collection amply reflects the many contrasting experiences of the three days of the Pope's visit. It is by no means an exercise in *plamás*. If anything, the collection contains a surprising number of sharp, critical, and in some cases extremely robust reactions to John Paul II's visit to Ireland.

13

Not everyone, by any means, applauds what the Pope said at Drogheda. One would not expect such applause from Danny Morrison, the Sinn Féin spokesman who memorably coined the phrase that the IRA proceeds by means of both the armalite and the ballot box – and one doesn't get it, either. For him, the Pope's approach was one-sided, ignoring loyalist violence – although I think it should be pointed out that the Ulster loyalists do not exactly form part of the Pope's constituency, and therefore he has no authority over them (as they, indeed, have tirelessly, even tediously, pointed out).

But other voices also express hostility towards the visit. Dan Keenan, the Northern news editor of the *Irish Times,* was little impressed by the Drogheda scene: 'I listened to his Drogheda sermon on the radio and his mispronounced plea to the paramilitaries to call it off. It wasn't convincing, and I'm not surprised they found him fit to ignore.' Nell McCafferty, that indefatigable Derrywoman, noted the incongruity between the papal plea 'on bended knees' and the visual evidence that the pontiff was actually sitting in a chair as he spoke. Not even papal infallibility could reconcile this contradiction, she writes. (It is usually Ulster Protestants who are accused of being a little too literal-minded, a little inflexible when it comes to metaphor and symbolic speech: Nell here puts herself squarely within that unimaginative tradition.)

It is left to Tim Pat Coogan, as a historian – and no admirer of John Paul II (he voices his 'distaste for [the Pope's] conservatism in matters affecting the reality of sexuality') – to grasp the significant point that the germ of the peace process in the North of Ireland was sown that day in Drogheda. On the face of things, the Troubles went on. Indeed, the melodrama of Bobby Sands's election to the House of Commons, his death, and the deaths of the other hunger strikers, was still to occur. Yet as with the scattering of the scriptural mustard seed, if some fell on barren ground and some was blown away by the wind, some, all the same, found a purchase in a fertile patch of earth and led, eventually, to regeneration.

The Bishop of Down and Conor, Cathal Daly, had, according to Mr Coogan, written much of the key Drogheda speech: an unsurprising revelation for anyone who has read Dr Daly's repeated sermons over the years, which constantly pleaded for peaceful means of political and social advance. And then, Gerry Adams did take cognisance. He began to ask what were the political means available to Sinn Féin. 'Eventually, the Redemportist priest Father Alex Reid realised the significance of what Adams was saying and doing,' Coogan writes. 'Perhaps the political route was opening up?' And thus, the embryonic phase of the peace process took shape – something for which we must indeed be thankful. When it eventually bore fruit in the Good Friday Agreement, Tim Pat Coogan toasted the Pope, after all, in Rome.

*

Criticism and hostility to John Paul II's 'conservatism in matters affecting sexuality' are not unusual in these texts. Danny Morrison, Nell McCafferty, David Norris and Ivana Bacik are among those who are sharply critical of the pontiff's traditionalism in this sphere. 'There was little to celebrate in the message that the Pope brought to Ireland,' writes Ms Bacik. She was eleven years old at the time, and already a radical feminist in some respects: she was the only girl in her liberal school in Dublin to express 'pro-choice' views in abortion debates.

The fact that she was the only pupil to hold such views openly at the time is itself an indicator of the solidity of traditional Irish values. Ms Bacik regards the papal message as 'condemnatory of those practising family planning, repressive of women and gay people, and dismissive of children.' The Ireland that has developed in the twenty-five years since then is, in her opinion, a 'more prosperous, multicultural and outward-looking place . . . Rights for gay people, Travellers and people with disabilities are increasingly becoming asserted through political lobbying and the passing of legislation.' Ivana Bacik, being a lawyer, has a strong sense of rights, but sometimes a shaky sense of social history: the Catholic Church in Ireland was actually the first agency to take up the cause of Travellers, as a trawl through the archives of religious magazines in the 1960s quickly reveals. As for people with disabilities, it was the abortion-rights lobby which aimed to eliminate people with disabilities from society altogether (see Simms and Hindell's *Abortion Law Reformed*, London, 1971: the standard text on the ideology of the pro-choice movement). And, *pace* Ms Bacik, the Pope said nothing at all about gay people during his visit to Ireland.

Nevertheless, Ivana Bacik's essay is feisty and spirited, and her general views are forcefully argued. Diversity and pluralism are indeed necessary elements in a free society, and I welcome the fact that a book marking the twenty-fifth anniversary of the papal visit to Ireland includes these notes of dissidence. Even Catholic Ireland of past times was not always as intolerant and rigid as it is painted: my very traditional Irish Catholic mother's favourite saying was: 'It would be a poor world if we were all the same', and that was a value she practised. My father, who very nearly became a Jesuit priest, said it in French: *'Chacun à son gout.'*

But just for the record, perhaps it is worth reporting precisely what John Paul II said about values and sexuality when he was in Ireland. In his Phoenix Park address, he warned against 'trends [of] present-day civilization and progress . . . The very capability of mass media to bring the whole world into your homes produces a . . . confrontation with values that until now have been alien to Irish society. Human identity is often defined by what one owns.' He did speak about the indissolubility of the marriage bond – which is standard Catholic doctrine – but his reference to contraception was quite delicate: marriage, he said, 'must include openness to the gift of children.' On abortion, he spoke of the importance of having 'an absolute and holy respect for the sacredness of human life from the first moment of its conception.' This ideal would certainly have been shared by the majority of the people at the time, as Ivana Bacik's schoolmates had already demonstrated to her.

*

But if some contributors here are critical, or even completely indifferent to the visit (one cannot but marvel at novelist Sheila O'Flanagan's ability to remain totally unmoved by what was occurring around her, although, in describing her fidelity to her own partner for twenty-five years, she is, paradoxically perhaps, an exemplar of the Pope's idealisation of marriage), many express the feeling of joy and excitement, and sense of historical moment, that they experienced. The pilot who brought John Paul to Ireland, Tommy McKeown, describes with exhilaration the unique sensation of flying over Dublin at 1,300 feet, and the million faces in Phoenix Park gazing up at the papal aircraft: 'As I look

16

back over twenty-five years, I feel privileged to have met the most dominant figure of the last century.'

The detective who protected the Holy Father, Tommy Farrell, felt similarly honoured. Liz Jackson, who, as a little girl, was chosen to present flowers to John Paul, will remember the occasion all her life, and describes it with unaffected simplicity. Bill Cullen, the Renault businessman and author, links the papal visit with the great Eucharistic Congress of 1932, when, as he so rightly says, working-class Catholics relied on their faith to get them through the vicissitudes of their hard lives. The broadcaster Joe Duffy recalls with vividness the 'outpourings of joy and fervour' generated by the Pope's visit, and Maeve Binchy comically describes how the Pope practically proved his infallibility by conjuring up serried ranks of telephones, which were suddenly installed in Phoenix Park. (Be it remembered that, in those times, a telephone was a very desirable, often long-desired object: to obtain one swiftly was near to being a miracle.)

Perhaps most touching of all is Ruth Buchanan's story. She writes of how she, as a Protestant, felt initially excluded from the preparations for the visit, and determined to ignore the whole event, and of how the sudden illness of her pooch brought about an emergency which had her, at the end of the day, moved to tears by it all. And very definitely included.

There are indeed many entries here which tell of joy, and echo Mary Banotti's exhilaration of the sense of 'bliss was it in that dawn to be alive', but it is quite appropriate that there should be those who cast a colder eye. Frank McGuinness's contribution is harshly critical, but he makes a point that should be heeded, and that is privately aired within the ranks of Catholic orthodoxy. Contemplating the Youth Mass in Galway, at which Bishop Eamonn Casey and Father Michael Cleary officiated, Mr McGuinness writes: 'If there is ever a moment when the Catholic Church is honest and admits how much it has brought about its own pain, it should look to that day and to those men. The hypocrisy is sickening.' (Although, *par contre*, Patsy McGarry considers Bishop Casey and Father Cleary to have been the most socially responsive of clerics in their concern for homelessness and issues of poverty.) All the same, many orthodox Catholics are asking, privately, whether the Pope's visit was used as a display of Catholic triumphalism rather than as an opportunity to examine honestly the problems which were already in the bud, and to think about reform and renewal.

This is a very important question, and it will be taken up by future historians. The papal visit of 1979 was the fulcrum of Irish Catholicism, and at the same time the signal of its ebb. The point needs to be made, but not strained: what churl among us would rain on the parade of those for whom it was a wonderful, joyful and quite literally never-to-be-repeated occasion?

For many centuries, Ireland kept the old faith, and it was, indeed, sometimes in spite of dungeon, fire and sword. For that long fidelity, Ireland deserved to be among the first countries that the Polish Pope would choose to visit; and she was. He alighted from the aircraft, looking, in Nell McCafferty's words, 'handsome, virile, gentle, happy and gorgeously dressed.' He descended the steps and kissed 'the old sod', recalls Sean McMahon. The sense of rapture that followed was, in Maeve Binchy's summing up, 'nothing to do with his being infallible or anything; it had everything to do with his having been here.' He was, in those glorious three days a quarter of a century ago, and for that we should remember and say hallelujah.

MARY KENNY is a journalist and the author of, among other books, *Goodbye to Catholic Ireland*, a social history of Ireland in the twentieth century, and, most recently, *Germany Calling*, an acclaimed biography of William Joyce, Lord Haw-Haw. She divides her life between Dublin and Kent.

'I DROPPED THE PAN AND GRABBED
THE NEAREST APPROXIMATION TO A FLAG'

It is a strange fact that one of the first sights that might have caught the Pope's attention as he arrived in Ireland was a red flag waved enthusiastically from a small boat that was hard aground in the River Liffey.

I had recently got a job in Kilkenny, and rather than keep my twenty-two-foot clinker-built cabin boat (not nearly grand enough to call a cruiser) in Dublin or on the Shannon, I decided to move her to the triple Nore-Barrow-Suir estuary near Waterford, where she would be only an hour's drive from our new home. Tired of canal travel, and knowing I had an ultra-reliable little diesel engine that would keep going if hell froze over, I found moorings in Dun Laoghaire harbour and was waiting for a combination of settled fair weather and convenient tides to start my harbour-to-harbour dashes down the coast and finally round the south-east corner of Ireland. My wife, Deirdre, and two of the children were determined to be in the Phoenix Park to greet the first Pope to set foot in Ireland, and our two plans meshed well. If I got the weather I wanted, I could start down the coast to Wicklow, and Deirdre could drive the car back, maybe picking me up from whatever harbour I had reached on the way.

On the day of the Pope's coming, there was good reason – I can't remember if it was weather or tide or both – not to start my trip, and I decided instead to join the crowds in Dublin. I slipped my moorings and headed across Dublin Bay and up the Liffey, listening to Radio Éireann as I went. To keep any hostile folk guessing, nobody knew where the Pope's plane was to make its landfall before coming in to Dublin Airport. I had just scraped under Capel Street Bridge and gone firmly aground above it, and was making a belated breakfast, when, the radio announced, the jumbo jet was spotted, heading straight up the Liffey from the sea. I looked up and there she was, gleaming in the silver, green and white Aer Lingus livery and flying at what seemed about fifty feet above the river, with a small jet plane escorting her at each wingtip. I'm sure she was really at least five hundred feet above the ground, but a jumbo jet at that height seems to fill the sky. She was a thrilling and majestic sight. I dropped the frying pan and grabbed the nearest approx-imation to a flag – which happened to be a bright-red beach towel – and waved it madly as the jumbo roared over me and began a steep turn over the million-odd people in the Park, only a mile upriver.

I then enjoyed my bacon and eggs while listening to the radio com-mentary and waiting for the tide to refloat me – much to the amusement of the Guards and others who were doing an extremely efficient job of marshalling buses to and from the Park on the quays beside me.

Jeremy Addis is the publisher of *Books Ireland*

'WE HAVE COME A LONG WAY

IN THE LAST TWENTY-FIVE YEARS'

I was eleven years old when the Pope visited Ireland in 1979. Just arrived up in Dublin for boarding school and away from my family in Cork, I was on childminding duty for all my younger cousins. My grandmother and both my uncles were living in Dublin with their families, and as the oldest grandchild I was a regular babysitter. So I was the obvious choice that day to help my grandmother in minding the small terrors, then ranging in age from three years down to a few months old. Other relatives departed to Phoenix Park for the great event, replete with picnic baskets, umbrellas and rosary beads; and there I was with my beloved gran, a baby on each knee and the toddlers staggering around the room, all of us watching with interest the immense pomp and ceremony that surrounded the Pope's arrival at the Park.

But there was little to celebrate in the message that the Pope brought to Ireland. The gospel that he preached, then as now, belonged to a hard and uncompromising Catholic faith, a rigid approach to doctrine unaffected by Vatican II reforms, condemnatory of those practising family planning, repressive of women and gay people, and dismissive of children. How appropriate to have watched him preaching that ungenerous message, while sitting at home minding the kids.

Even then, influenced by my parents, I was sceptical about what the Pope's visit represented. Although we were all brought up Catholic, my parents had always been distrustful of the intolerant, hardline approach to morality taken by the Pope and many of the Irish Catholic hierarchy, and they did not make the journey to see the Pope speak.

Four years after the Pope's visit, Ireland was embroiled in a bitter referendum campaign precipitated by the anti-abortion movement, which had campaigned for constitutional protection for the foetus. I remember arguing against the amendment while in my class at school: even at a liberal all-girls' school in Dublin, it was difficult and unpopular to take a pro-choice position. The referendum was carried, and today our Constitution still guarantees the foetus an equal right to life with that of the pregnant woman. Apart from the symbolic devaluing of women's lives that this represents, the same referendum has generated an immense amount of litigation, in which I later became involuntarily involved.

Ten years after the Pope's visit, as the elected President of Trinity College Students' Union, I and a group of other students'-union officers were threatened with prison under the 1983 constitutional amendment because we had provided information on abortion to women in crisis pregnancy: we had given out the phone number of an underground non-directive counselling helpline. A number of women's clinics had already been closed down on the same basis, and the students' unions were the only organisations willing to defy the law by that time. Because of this, every day we received desperate, panicky phone calls from women in crisis pregnancy, of all ages, from all over Ireland. All of these women were denied access to information they needed about a medical procedure that was legally available just across the Irish Sea. Fortunately for us, Mary Robinson, then a Senior Counsel, took on our defence, along with a brave and hard-working legal team, and we escaped prison when the High Court referred our case to the European Court of Justice.

By the time the case had been ruled upon there, and had been finally resolved in the Irish courts, it was 1996, and public attitudes had moved on significantly. The election of Mary Robinson as President in 1990, the legalisation of contraception in the early 1990s, the X case in 1992 and the carrying of the divorce referendum in 1995 all brought about, or marked significant shifts in, attitudes, views and practices, and contributed to liberalisation and progression in Irish society.

Now, twenty-five years after the Pope's visit, Ireland is a more prosperous, multicultural and outward-looking place. We no longer have net emigration: people actually want to come and live here. Contraceptives are legally available, and women no longer have to scribble phone numbers for underground abortion information helplines on the backs of toilet doors. Rights for gay people, Travellers, children and people with disabilities are increasingly becoming asserted through political lobbying and the passing of legislation. Of course, much more needs to be done to bring about a truly equal, pluralist and tolerant society in Ireland, in which each individual is valued on their own merits. But we have come a long way in the last twenty-five years. The Pope would not recognise Irish society as it is today. His views and values may not have changed over that time, but thankfully ours have – greatly for the better.

IVANA BACIK is a practising barrister and the Reid Professor of Criminal Law, Criminology and Penology at Trinity College Dublin

'THE FIRST POPE WHO EVER LEFT ROME'

I had been on holiday in Italy for a week prior to the Pope's visit and came home on the last flight from Rome before the airport was closed in preparation for the Pope's journey to Ireland. We arrived in late, to an amazingly quiet Dublin, and fell asleep believing that our trip to Rome was sufficient exposure to the Vatican.

I woke early in the morning and lay in bed thinking about the amazing event of the Pope's visit. I decided to take out my bike and cycle to the Park, even though I had made no arrangements and had no idea what I might do when I got there. It was a beautiful day, and as I cycled through the empty streets I remember thinking how lucky I was to live in such a beautiful city.

I got to the edge of the Park, and everywhere there was a sense of gaiety and goodwill. A nice man insisted I park my bike, and as I bade goodbye to it I was certain that by the time I eventually returned it would have been stolen, as had all its predecessors. I found myself at the very back of the corrals and had a very fleeting glimpse of the Popemobile and a fuzzy view of the altar. I have a primitive fear of being in very large crowds, but my abiding memory of that day is of a vast, good-humoured national picnic. No drunks, no transistor radios, no pushing and shoving – rather a universal sense that, for most of the people there, this was the most special and unexpected event in the country.

I had seen thousands of Irish people over the years arriving with the spring in Rome, weighted down with plastic bags and that special pilgrimage feeling which characterised so many of them during the sixties and seventies. Anyone I ever spoke to in Rome, including my mother and aunts, from Ireland was shocked and amazed by how few Italians ever went to daily Mass. I remember my mother and aunt hardly being off their knees for the entire duration of their visit, and now 'Here was the Pope coming to visit us!'

For the older generation, he was the first Pope who ever left Rome; certainly for the first twenty-four hours of his visit, when it was still running to schedule, he fulfilled everyone's breathless expectations. When the event finished and everyone started moving off in regular, peaceful, ordered lines, I slipped neatly through the crowds, retrieved

my bike and, for the first and last time, cycled through the beautiful traf-
fic-free city to my house in Ringsend.

MARY BANOTTI is a Fine Gael politician and the European Parliament
President's Mediator for Transnationally Abducted Children

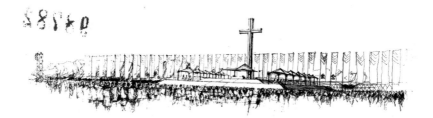

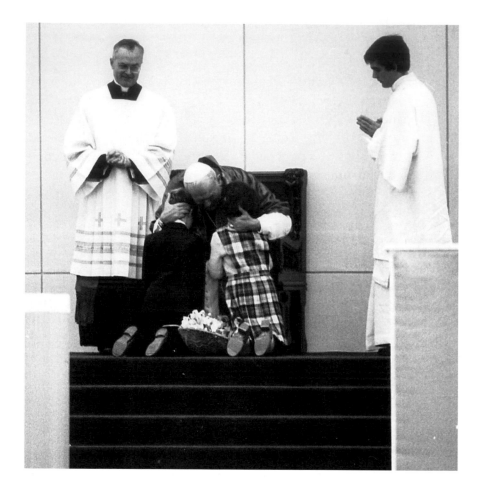

'I KNEW IT WOULD PAY OFF EVENTUALLY BEING A NUN'

In the May of 1979 I went for the *Irish Times* to Mayo to write about Knock. Canon Horan showed me where the Pope's helicopter was going to land when he came to visit. I'm afraid I thought the Canon was barking mad. The Pope come to *Ireland*? To *Knock*? Oh, please. Anyway, the Canon was right and I was wrong, and the Pope did come at the end of the summer. And the whole country went mad.

We were up at the crack of dawn the day he was arriving, and we went in a line of journalists' buses to the Phoenix Park. In those days, you couldn't get a new phone for love nor money, but they had managed to install a thousand phones in the Park in five weeks, so now we knew it actually was possible, and the phone people never got away with anything again.

It was very dark as the buses full of godless journalists crept along beside the faithful who were walking to the Park. There were huge tents waiting for us, some of them fairly specialized, like the one with the heading 'Bishops Vesting'. A colleague, Sean MacReamoinn from RTÉ, was standing outside that tent with his microphone and tape recorder, saying 'Bishops Vesting, One Two Three', which we thought was hysterically funny at five in the morning.

Then the dawn came out and we came out of the 'Breakfast Tent' to see how many people had turned up, and harder souls than mine were overtaken by the gulp factor as we saw more than one and a third million people gathered to welcome the Pope. A third of the population. We didn't use the word 'awesome' then, but that's exactly what it was.

Oh, there were great facilities altogether for us. There was even a big Portaloo which said 'Ladies of the Press' on the door.

A small, worried nun came in and wondered could she be allowed in. 'It's really meant to be for the Ladies of the Press, Sister,' said the attendant. 'But seeing that it's yourself, please consider yourself very welcome.'

'I knew it would pay off eventually being a nun,' the little Sister said, delighted with herself, and with the day that lay ahead.

We wandered around looking at the people who had come from all over the land. Invalids in wheelchairs were in ranks near the front, all of them with big laminated photo identification. One old man had a picture of his cottage and himself and his sheepdog. He looked like a speck in the picture: there was no way that it identified him at all.

But I thought of the basic humanity of whoever had been checking him in, someone with the kindness to realise that this old man wasn't a terrorist going to kill the Pope and that he probably only *had* one picture of himself, taken from the gate by a visiting cousin from America. He sat with his rosary, smiling with happiness and anticipation, and I had to go away and have a big weep behind 'Bishops Vesting' to get over it all.

And then the priest who was doing the warm-up said that the Holy Father had now entered Irish airspace, and one and a third million people cheered to the echo. I hoped I wasn't going to spend the entire day crying into my picnic lunch.

The day just seemed to fly by, and everyone was good-tempered, and the Pope was very near, and everyone said he smiled at them directly, which was great.

That night we were in a pub in Fleet Street opposite the *Irish Times*, all of us glued to the television. 'His Holiness has just come into Sean MacDermott Street,' the television said.

'He'd want to watch his handbag there,' someone said from the crowd.

And we all went to bed exhausted, knowing we had to get up at four to catch the train to Knock.

I avoided Canon Horan's eye, I was so ashamed of ever doubting him.

They had turned the Confession boxes into phone boxes: ours said *Irish Times, Boston Globe* and *Le Soir*. We all took photos of each other leaning out of them.

I'm not very holy, and there are many things I wish the Pope had said or hadn't said over the years, but only a terrible curmudgeon would not have enjoyed that buzzy, happy visit.

It had nothing to do with his being infallible or anything; it had everything to do with his having been here.

MAEVE BINCHY is the author, most recently, of *Night of Rain and Stars*

'While I pretended to sleep, they had sex'

It was a time of innocence; it was a time of denial. There were words which had no significance then. Words like Granard, the Darkley Hall, Greysteel, Annie Murphy, the X case, the C case, Goldenbridge, Michael Fortune, Brendan Smyth.

It was a time of innocence and denial for me too. I was thirteen, and a late developer. When my friends were discovering the musky pleasures of courting, I just wanted to play with my bike and stage battles with hordes of imaginary enemies in my back garden. In my second year at St Enda's Community School, the first two weeks of term were dominated by arrangements for the visit of John Paul II. A skier, a playwright, a goalie! Karol Wojtyla, the young Polish Pope, coming to Limerick?

Well, at fifty-nine he didn't seem that young to me. And I was a little atheist. I never got a proper answer to the question: if God made the world, then who made God? So I had set my head against religion and all its works. I had secretly given up going to Mass and had decided that I would not be joining His Holiness at Limerick Racecourse prior to his departure for Rome. Events were to conspire to bring us together, in spite of my indifference.

I was lured by the great adventure of a night under the stars amid the tumult. I also had a mission. The critical thing for the great throng of believers was to find oneself on the route that the Popemobile would take around the park after Mass. This route was a closely guarded secret: how was a young boy to get his hands on such classified intelligence? The Limerick Civil Defence knew the route: they had a map. I found myself in possession of a copy of a copy of a copy of that map.

I was a hero. Our secret percolated through the neighbourhood's youth: our numbers had swelled to twenty by the time we set off on our epic journey from the South Circular Road to the Green Park Racecourse. Actually, Green Park Racecourse was *on* the South Circular Road, so we didn't have far to walk, but the journey at 3 AM with hordes of other people was a bizarre and eerie experience. It felt like we were going to a football match or a big concert, but the mood of the crowd was workmanlike. There was busy-ness in the air. We were attending to matters of great import. This was the Church triumphant, a valediction of the generations that had committed our state to Mother Rome. The demeanour of the Limerick crowd was in marked contrast to the ecstatic scenes we had witnessed after John Paul's visit to the seminary in Maynooth, where the Pope was greeted as a superstar. Delighted young clerics, drunk on the proximity of real divinity, shoved forward to clutch the hem of his garments. There was no such hysteria in Redemptorist Limerick. We knew how to behave ourselves in church, or at the racecourse, or both.

At the venue, confusion reigned. We couldn't work out which gate we had come in through, and could not make out significant landmarks in the dark. My popularity ebbed, we got tired and cranky, and eventually gave up the search until daybreak. We set up camp we knew not where.

Nearby were some men and women in their early twenties. They had bottles of wine with them, smoked Major cigarettes and chatted. They offered us cigarettes, which we accepted manfully, and we debated which direction the Pope's helicopter would appear from. We showed them our map. They resolved to help us in the morning, telling us not to show the map to anyone else. We felt better now that there were adults on the case, and cool ones at that!

Then we all got into our sleeping bags. A young man and a young woman doubled theirs up and got in together. Then, right next to me, while I pretended to sleep, they had sex. I acknowledge that, if someone else had written this as fiction, I would dismiss it as being too blatant, too consciously ironic. But it happened. It was my first real sexual experience, only I didn't have it. They were discreet, and I didn't dare draw anyone else's attention to the occurrence, because I didn't want them to stop. I wanted to see what would happen.

As dawn spread across the sky and they slept, I gazed at them – or more particularly at the young woman. I felt I had been admitted to a new world. I felt grown up.

Hours passed uneventfully. The muffled sounds of a giant campsite grew louder as more and more of the congregation emerged from beneath their covers blinking into the morning light. At 7 AM, the PA started broadcasting Irish country and western music. This was our call to prayer. Then, at 8 AM, our council of war convened. We knew where we were. We could see the giant altar. We were to the right of it. We deciphered the magic map. We only had to move five hundred yards to be on the route. Chinese whispers spread among the group, and we moved in pairs or threes so as not to draw attention to ourselves. I was rewarded with a sandwich and a hug from my new best friend, the scarlet lady. I had a radio and was able to track the Pope's progress towards Limerick. Then we heard the blades of the helicopter in the distance. I remember seeing a white figure waving down at the crowd. I waved back.

I had one last trick up my sleeve. As the Pope spoke, his words were transmitted live on local radio. The radio received the signal and broadcast it to my ear before the sound signal reached us from the PA. So, by holding the radio to my ear, I was able to speak the Pope's lines to the crowd around me, before they heard them from his own mouth. I thought this was hilarious. The crowd around me thought I was being disrespectful and confiscated my radio.

I don't recall much of what the Pope said. I remember him mentioning the evils of contraception, and watching the young lovers for signs of guilt. They showed none – but then neither did Bishop Eamonn Casey or Father Michael Cleary at Ballybrit.

Then the Pope did his lap of honour. The map was correct, and we were in an ideal spot. I meant to keep the map as a souvenir, but I think one of the grown-ups held on to it. I wonder where they are now, and whether they still have it.

What did it all mean? Well, I think that for Ireland as a nation it meant a lot that the Pope came to Ireland and told us that he loved us. I think we needed to hear that: we needed to feel loved, wanted and special. In fact, I think we behaved like an abandoned child during a rare visit of our usually absent father.

The gleeful triumphalism of the Irish clerical hierarchy was in marked contrast to the apparent humility of the Holy Father. This land is our land, they proclaimed, but of course they didn't know about those words, full of religious resonance, that lay in the future: Granard, the Darkley Hall, Greysteel, Annie Murphy, the X case, the C case, Goldenbridge, Michael Fortune, Brendan Smyth.

JOHN BREEN is the author of *Alone It Stands,* among other plays

41

'SMILING BROADLY, THE POPE SAID:
"GOD BLESS EUROPE"'

Along with hundreds of journalists, I packed into the concert hall of the Dominican Convent in Cabra on the first night of the Pope's visit. There I heard that a special meeting between the government and the pontiff was to take place across the road at the Nunciature, the residence of the Papal Nuncio. I wanted to get in on that to witness what I anticipated would be the cowering obeisance of the Catholic rulers of a Catholic state before Christ's representative on earth.

To my surprise, there wasn't much trouble getting in. I was a little disappointed to see the spouses present: this signaled that the encounter with the pontiff would be less formal, and perhaps less secret, than I had hoped. There was a small unmanned camera on a tripod in a corner of the room, which I assumed was there to record the encounter for posterity.

I joined Charles Haughey, then Minister for Health and Social Welfare and soon to be Taoiseach, and Brian Lenihan, who was also a minister at the time. Their demeanour seemed less reverential than I expected from Catholic ministers awaiting the arrival of their supreme ruler. The Pope was running late, and the Papal Nuncio had assuaged the impatience of these important people with regularly refreshed glasses of spirits and wine. It showed: there was a fairly light-hearted atmosphere in the room.

After quite a wait, the Pope showed up, looking very tired and irritable. Jack Lynch read a speech at him, badly. Then the Pope read a speech at the government ministers, badly, and went around the room shaking hands. He was introduced to the ministers and their spouses by Lynch, rather as the captain of an Irish football team introduces players to the deputy Lord Mayor of Dublin at Lansdowne Road on important occasions. Except that Lynch couldn't remember the names of his ministers and their spouses. He signalled that they should introduce themselves. The Pope shook my hand, presumably in the belief that I was one of the rulers of the Catholic state – not that by that stage he could have cared less.

43

The Pope exited, as did the ministers and their spouses. I thought I would hang on, because the Diplomatic Corps was to be introduced to the Pope immediately afterwards. Their Excellencies were crowded into the hallway just outside the room. By this stage, I was on my own in the room. I could see that there was some agitation among their Excellencies, possibly to do with the order in which they would enter the room and therefore the order in which they would be introduced to the Pope. Eventually their Excellencies came into the room in a line, led, I think, by the Nigerian ambassador, dressed in full African costume. He did a full tour of the room and joined me opposite the door. He thought I was someone important.

Last to arrive was Richard Burke, then Ireland's European Commissioner. He was the only person there whom I recognised and I was the only person there whom he recognised. Risking another diplomatic incident, he came over to stand beside me at the front of the line, instead of staying at the back. There was a little tut-tutting, but nothing more serious.

The Pope came back in. This time he was very irritable, very bored and very tired. Someone read a speech at him: it might have been my friend the Nigerian ambassador. The Pope read a speech at them and then went around the room shaking hands again, but in the wrong order. He came to Dick Burke and myself. Burke, introducing himself to the Pope, said: 'Richard Burke, Europe.' The Pope's eyes momentarily lit up. Smiling broadly, he said: 'God bless Europe.' He had not offered any such salutation to anybody else that I noticed.

He then turned to me, with a vague recollection that he had seen me a short while previously. I thought for a moment that I should explain, but then thought better of it. He left, and I rejoined my journalistic colleagues across the road in the Dominican Convent. When the Pope finally appeared on the balcony overlooking the hall, the journalists went shamefully delirious, singing over and over: 'He's got the whole world in his hands.' The Pope seemed to like that.

*

The camera in the corner of the room where we met the Pope in the Nunciature was a television camera. The secret meetings with the ministers and their Excellencies were broadcast live. Brian Farrell did a commentary, I assume from a studio at RTÉ. He identified me as Bobby Molloy. I have never forgotten that, or forgiven it. Neither has Bobby Molloy.

VINCENT BROWNE is a writer and broadcaster; his current-affairs magazine *The Village* will be launched in October

'WHERE DO YOU FIND A VET

ON THE DAY THE POPE IS IN DUBLIN?'

It was a glorious summer day.

It wasn't, of course. It was the end of September. But the sun was shining and the entire population of Dublin was in festival mood.

Most citizens got up at five o'clock that day. They packed their sandwiches, put on their most comfortable shoes, gathered up their raincoats, and off they went.

Through the streets they teemed, walking miles and miles and miles, the strong helping the weak, the small high on their fathers' shoulders, the young urging their elders to step on it.

We felt a bit left out. A bit like we used to before the GAA became ecumenical, when Protestants weren't really regarded as Irish. It wasn't our day.

Oh yes, we Anglicans have a leader but, somehow, the title 'Archbishop of Canterbury' doesn't have quite the same ring to it, does it? He is not referred to as 'Your Holiness'. Still, we will, almost certainly, one day refer to our leader as 'Her Grace'. I will not live to hear the words 'Her Holiness'.

Okay, I admit it: I was jealous. I *was* put out that day. We weren't part of it and, to rub salt in the wound, we had given a bed to some Northern Irish Catholic friends of ours who arrived with their five children and oozed jollity and ecumenism and got us up at four o'clock in the morning to wave them and their two double-buggies off.

We skulked back into the house to be greeted by our new pup, who skipped and licked and wagged her tail. She liked Prods, particularly *these* Prods, who hadn't abandoned her in favour of the Pope.

She had arrived only two days before and was still nameless. But she had felt enough at home to eat our son's Action Man, pee on my husband's socks, and devour the chicken-liver pâté I had made for our Northern Irish friends.

Still, she was our little pet and we loved her, so we forgave her all and brought her out to the garden to play ball. We were determined to ignore what was happening in the Phoenix Park.

47

The day passed happily enough, with just the occasional sneaky glance at the events on the telly, which were of no real interest to us at all. Or so we pretended.

And then it happened. 'Nameless' collapsed and spluttered and choked. I knew she was going to die because I knew she had parvovirus and distemper and hepatitis and leptospirosis and all the things that kill puppies who haven't been vaccinated.

A vet. We needed a vet. In the name of God, where do you find a vet on the day the Pope is in Dublin?

We found one. We rang the Veterinary Hospital and were told that two vets were on duty that day, one on the northside and one on the southside. The vet told us that the only thing wrong with Nameless was the pâté she had eaten. He gave her a jab and told us to take her home and keep her quiet.

And that is how we ended up sitting comfortably, cuddling our new pup and absolutely glued to the television for three whole days. And when the Pope said: 'Young people of Galway, I love you', I cried.

RUTH BUCHANAN is the presenter of *Playback* on RTÉ Radio 1

'A VERY DECENT SPUD'

From childhood, I have had an aversion to pomp and parade. Brought up in the Bible Belt of north Down, I sang in the church choir, parading from vestry to choir stalls in surplice and cassocks, Matins and Evensong, every Sunday. Out on the streets during the long school holidays, the parades seemed unending, with miles of Orangemen following the banners of King William crossing the Boyne and Queen Victoria handing the Bible to the Suppliant Negro, and the bands, the flutes, the pipes, the drums, all proclaiming: 'No Pope Here'. I migrated in the 1950s to what my mother always called the Free State, leaving behind not only the pandemic bigotry of those long summers, but any vestige of religious belief that might have survived those Sundays in the choir stalls.

So when, thirty-five years after my voice broke, the Pope came to Dublin, I was not among the great crowds who made their way to the airport or the Phoenix Park. But I watched it on the telly on and off, and when the action moved to Drogheda, I watched every moment. But this is not, I fear, the story of a Pauline conversion. In fact, I was paying less attention to the Pope than to the lovely handwoven tapestry that hung behind him. This tapestry, with its device of the papal keys, was designed and woven by my wife, Helena Ruuth, on a vast and wonderful Irish hand-loom. Helena had been brought from Sweden to Ireland to help set up the woven-textiles section of the newly established Kilkenny Design Centre. Now freelance, she had been commissioned by the Irish Tapestry Company of Drogheda to create the tapestry, which hangs now in St Peter's Church in Drogheda.

We of course made a videotape of the Drogheda visit, and visitors to our house over the next weeks were subjected to endless replays. In the twenty-five years since then, and more especially this year, the 1979 visit has been recalled on television, featuring almost always the picture of the Pope standing before the tapestry, and we all shout at each other to come and look, and smile with sinful pride.

I even know now, after all those replays, what the Pope actually said that day in Drogheda. Just weeks after the terrible murders at Mullaghmore and Warrenpoint, he spoke to the politicians, to the young people and their parents, and to the murderers themselves, begging them, on his knees, to turn away from violence:

> You may claim to seek justice. I, too, believe in justice, and seek justice. But violence only delays the day of justice. Violence destroys the work of justice. Further violence in Ireland will only drag down to ruin the land you claim to love and the values you claim to cherish.

Anyone reading these words today, in disembodied form, might feel entitled to dismiss them as mere public piety. But in the many times since then that I have heard them spoken on screen, I have come to see them as a true expression of grief, of shared suffering.

What I came to like most about the man who spoke them, in spite of my mistrust of the robe and the splendour, the pomp and the parade, was his air of the common man. I thought he seemed a very decent spud.

WESLEY BURROWES writes for film and television; he is perhaps best known for his work on the long-running RTÉ soap opera *Glenroe*

'HERE WAS A PHYSICAL-FORCE SPOKESMAN

TALKING POLITICS'

I must have been one of the very few people invited to meet the Pope on his visit to Ireland who did not take up the invitation. The 'meeting' would have taken place at a gathering for the press on the Navan Road which, in reality, would have constituted little more than an indoor, Irish version of the pontiff's appearances on the balcony in St Peter's Square. While this would of course have brought me a lot closer to the Pope's forcefield than the vast majority of those who saw him at Dublin, Drogheda, Galway and Limerick, my distaste for his conservatism in matters affecting the reality of human sexuality made me loath to abandon my garden for a closer look at the 'Man in White'.

Nearly twenty years later, however, outside Rome, at Castel Gandolfo, I found myself lifting a glass to toast John Paul, not for his theology, I hasten to add, but because what I learned on my visit to Italy that week had gone too far to confirm my hunch, formed over the years, that his visit to Ireland could come to be regarded as a significant milestone in the peace process.

What the world remembers of the papal address at Drogheda is the passage that commanded most attention at the time. It was directed at the IRA:

> Believe in peace and forgiveness, for they are of Christ. On my knees I beg you to turn away from the paths of violence and return to the ways of peace. You may claim to seek justice. I too believe in justice and seek justice. But violence only delays the day of peace. Violence destroys the work of justice . . . Do not follow any leaders who train you in the ways of inflicting death. Those who resort to violence always claim that only violence brings change. You must know that there is a political, peaceful way to justice.

Fairly predictably, the IRA rejected the appeal, which was widely seen by socialists and republicans as a concealed endorsement of the SDLP's position. The controversy which the rejection caused almost completely obscured the significance of another passage in the speech which was destined to provide the springboard to the peace process:

> To all who bear political responsibility for the affairs of Ireland, I want to speak with the same urgency and intensity with which I have spoken of the men of violence. Do not cause or condone conditions which give excuse or pretext for violence. Those who resort to violence always claim that only violence brings about change. They claim that political action cannot achieve justice. You politicians must prove them wrong. You must show them that there is a peaceful, political way to justice. You must show that peace achieves the work of justice.

With the delivery of that speech, there began a process of megaphone, unacknowledged debate in which the then Bishop of Down and Conor, Cathal Daly, apparently took up the position espoused in the first-quoted paragraph and Gerry Adams challenged various public utterances of the bishop on that theme, while at the same time advocating the sort of thinking expressed by the Pope in the second-quoted paragraph. Adams wanted to know what were the political means available to Sinn Féin, which at the time was banned from the airwaves, and also challenged the bishop to outline the Church's attitude towards the British occupation of the Six Counties and the methods used to maintain that occupation.

What few people realised at the time was that both paragraphs were written by the same man, the author of the speech, Cathal Daly. Prior to the Pope's visit, Daly had lived for a period in the Irish College in Rome, travelling up and down to Castel Gandolfo regularly with various drafts of the address the Pope would eventually deliver at Drogheda.

Eventually, however, the Redemptorist priest Father Alex Reid realised the significance of what Adams was saying and doing. Here was a physical-force spokesman talking politics. Perhaps the political route was opening up? After satisfying himself in consultation with the Redemptorist theologian Father Sean O'Riordan as to the propriety of Adams's questions to the bishop, he and Adams began the conversations which led to a wide variety of other figures, including myself, being brought into the process.

The way was long and filled with setbacks. For example, in an effort to bring the republicans into the mainstream of politics and away from violence, the late Cardinal Tomas Ó Fiaich agreed to meet publicly with the then pariah Gerry Adams. But the Cardinal died of a heart attack while on a pilgrimage to Lourdes. John Major was, in effect, politically castrated by his dependence on the Ulster Unionists in the House of Commons. Charlie Haughey refused to make a public move.

But Father Reid persisted. So did elements of the British mandarin class. The Hume-Adams dialogue developed. Albert Reynolds came to power. The Kennedys came aboard and ultimately, on 31 August 1994, the IRA agreed to a ceasefire. Although more difficulties were in store, the seeds sown on those journeys between the Irish College and Castel Gandolfo had borne fruit and the Good Friday Agreement was born.

So, though I had boycotted him in Ireland, I toasted the Pope in Italy.

TIM PAT COOGAN is the author, most recently, of *On the Blanket: The Inside Story of the IRA Prisoners' "Dirty" Protest*

'MANY YOUNGSTERS WENT WELL BEYOND

A HANDSHAKE AS A SIGN OF PEACE'

Is it a sin to lie about your age? If it is, then I blame you, Holy Father, for creating such an occasion on which I sinned, especially as I told my little porkie so I could get to see you say Mass in Galway.

Believe me, though, it was your fault for not coming to Cork. You may not have heard of the city – although most of us believed that you should have. That was a grievous insult to the people of the second city of this country, and an inconvenience to boot. Of course, you went to Dublin – everyone goes to Dublin, as the people of Cork well know – but you went to Drogheda, Knock, Limerick and Galway too, and not to Cork.

Excuse me while I digress for a few paragraphs, but this has been a topic of some disquiet in Cork for a quarter of a century now. For years afterwards, we expected you to return, to right that wrong. The *Cork Examiner,* as it was known then, regularly predicted your second coming to these shores, with a visit to Cork being the priority. But it never happened, even when you returned time after time to the same spots throughout the world.

Even now, when you're expected back in Ireland early in 2005, the talk is of a visit to the Six Counties because the North got left out the last time. Yes, and so did the South, but nobody seems too worried about that. You must be getting bad advice. But let me return to why I lied about my age twenty-five years ago.

*

Now, I was an innocent young boy at the time, just thirteen and in my second year at the North Monastery in Cork, a strict, tough Christian Brothers-led establishment. I'd done the altar-boy thing – and escaped the unwanted attentions of one or two priests too, I should say, not quite understanding then what they were after – and now took up church collections or did the readings at Mass. Your visit was important to me at the time but my parents didn't have a car and they opted for television coverage rather than a trip to far-away Limerick or elsewhere on public transport.

There was a chance to get to Galway, however. Our local church had hooked up with another parish to provide buses for 'the young people' to go west. A very early start one morning and a late return was envisaged for those over sixteen years of age. Which, clearly, I wasn't.

So, along with two of my friends – both aged fourteen, it should be said – I decided that nothing would stop my intention to be devout and pious. We lied about our age to gain access to the bus. Our parents, bless them, were complicit in this deception, and while they were doubtful about allowing us travel, they reckoned that there was no safer place for their children to go than to a Youth Mass. If only they knew what would really go on at Galway: it was a real eye-opener for someone of my age.

At the Youth Mass, I looked out over Ballybrit Racecourse to a wave of cheering by teenagers and young adults who didn't seem to know when to shut up, whipped up by the enthusiastic prompting of those later-to-be-revealed fornicators Eamonn Casey and Michael Cleary (dual fathers the both of them, so to speak). Maybe it was subconscious knowledge of what the pair of them were really up to, or maybe it was all the talk of loving each other, but – and this, to the best of my knowledge, went unreported at the time – many youngsters went well beyond a handshake as a sign of peace.

To a thirteen-year-old who wasn't allowed to go to discos – strict parenting in those days, don't you know – the sight of others 'making out' was quite revealing. Not, I may say, that I saw anyone going 'all the way', but the intentions were obvious – and may have been brought to fulfilment later that evening. I didn't exactly bow my head in prayer: I was too busy watching what was going on.

Later, I was to find another reason why I shouldn't have bothered lying. The buses were hours late departing Ballybrit because of the traffic jam. I consumed a bag of vinegar-saturated chips – which was not the fine cuisine to which my delicate tummy was subjected by my mother – as well as loads of fizzy drinks and a couple of chocolate bars, practice for my student days, which were still four years away.

I eventually fell asleep in the early hours of the morning and had to rely on my friends to tell me what happened next. Apparently, I started sleepwalking, wandering around the bus muttering to myself, before banging on a window and shouting 'Let me out!' I'm told that, when I was restrained, I responded by vomiting over one of the real sixteen-year-olds who was trying to put manners on me. Worse, I didn't even have the excuse that my sad performance was the result of my first feed of alcohol. Needless to say, when I eventually got home I had to tell a lot of lies to explain the state of my clothes, and of myself. But this was coming more naturally to me now that I was a fully fledged teenager, hardened by the experience of the past days.

And after all, if I had lied to see the Pope, then I could lie about anything.

MATT COOPER was the editor of the *Sunday Tribune* between 1996 and 2002 and now presents *The Last Word* news and current-affairs programme on Today FM

'The Ford Special Vehicle Operations team
went into action'

The visit of Pope John Paul to Ireland in September 1979 was flagged
very early to our family. For two unique reasons.

At the time of Pope John Paul's visit, we had our new Fairlane Ford
car dealership in Tallaght and we got the word twelve months in
advance, of the need for a special vehicle for the visit of His Holiness. A
small bus to carry himself and his close entourage in comfort but with
an upstairs pulpit-type balcony so he could bless and wave to the congregation. The Ford Special Vehicle Operations team went into action,
and the Popemobile was created. It was painted in the Pope's yellow and
white colours, with the Vatican logo of the keys to the Eternal City on
each side. The Popemobile was based at our premises in Tallaght and of
course acted as a showroom traffic-builder for a few weeks. Everyone
who bought a car got their photo with the Popemobile. Commercialism
knows no bounds.

Linked to Pope John Paul's visit was an event of forty-seven years
before. Back in 1932, the Da was part of the religious team co-ordinat-
ing the ceremonies in the Phoenix Park for the visit of the Papal
Nuncio, Pascal Robinson. The Cullen family were staunch Catholic
churchgoers, getting their Mass every morning, and the Da was the sacristan in the Pro-cathedral in Marlborough Street. Every evening he was
down in the church, wearing his long black priest-like cassock, preparing the altars for the Sodalities, the Novenas and the High Masses.
Preparing for the myriad religious ceremonies that were conducted in
the busy inner-city churches of that time. Working-class Dubliners rely-
ing on their Catholic faith to get them through the tough times of this
world, earning their passport to the happiness of heaven.

Not only was the Da an experienced organiser of church ceremonies, he was also an ex-Irish Free State army soldier. As it was the
army who were in charge of the logistics for the visit, the Da became a
useful go-between for the famous Lord Mayor of Dublin, Alfie Byrne.
If Alfie needed to readjust anything – seating layouts, VIP areas, holding
arenas – the Da was the ideal facilitator, as he knew the army guys and

was in the religious team too. He had always told us kids about the magical days back in '32 when he was Alfie Byrne's Supremo in the Park. The Ma called it his claim to fame, but to this day I have the letter of commendation given by Alfie on his Mansion House letterhead acknowledging Billy Cullen's service at the event. You can put that in your pipe and smoke it, Missus Cullen.

So, thanks to my Popemobile connections, I was able to get my parents the privilege of front-row seating at the Pope John Paul ceremony in the Phoenix Park. We had a chauffeur-driven limousine to glide up to the VIP enclosure. It was the thrill of a lifetime for them when the Pope rubbed his thumb on their foreheads after Holy Communion. Wasn't it a great thing to have two soldiers of Christ among the celebrities? Ordinary working-class Dubs, with an unbendable faith in the Church, Pioneers in Father Matthews' Total Abstinence Society, who could now tell all their friends about the day they met the Pope.

BILL CULLEN is the chairman of Renault Ireland and author of the best-selling memoir *It's a Long Way from Penny Apples*

'WHO YA GOT THERE, THE MAYOR?'

After getting all of Pope John Paul's luggage loaded into the limousine (he doesn't travel light), the driver notices that the Pope is still standing on the kerb.

'Excuse me, Your Eminence,' says the driver, 'would you please take your seat so we can leave?'

'Well, to tell you the truth,' says the Pope, 'they never let me drive at the Vatican, and I'd really like to drive today.'

'I'm sorry, but I can't let you do that. I'd lose my job! And what if something should happen?' protests the driver, wishing he'd never gone to work that morning.

'There might be something extra in it for you,' says the Pope.

Reluctantly, the driver gets in the back as the Pope climbs in behind the wheel. The driver quickly regrets his decision when, after exiting the airport, the Supreme Pontiff floors it, accelerating to 105 MPH.

'Please slow down, Your Holiness!' pleads the worried driver, but the Pope keeps the pedal to the metal until they hear sirens.

'Oh, dear God, I'm gonna lose my licence,' moans the driver.

The Pope pulls over and rolls down the window as the cop approaches, but the cop takes one look at him, goes back to his motorcycle, and gets on the radio.

'I need to talk to the Chief,' he says to the dispatcher.

The Chief gets on the radio and the cop tells him that he's stopped a limo going a hundred and five.

'So bust him,' says the Chief.

'I don't think we want to do that, he's really important,' replies the cop.

The Chief exclaims: 'All the more reason!'

'No, I mean *really* important,' says the cop.

The Chief asks: 'Who ya got there, the Mayor?'

'Bigger.'

'The Governor?'

'Bigger.'

'Okay,' says the Chief, 'who is it?'

'I think it's God!'

'What makes you think it's God?' the Chief asks.
'He's got the Pope for a chauffeur.'

ANNE DUDLEY

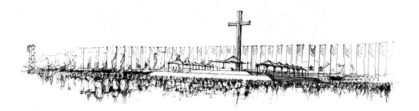

'THE GREAT MAN FROM POLAND'

Firstly I was told it was my accent that got me the spot on the Papal Altar at the Galway Youth Mass. Then one journalist told me that I got the offer because I happened to be president of Trinity Students' Union - and it was an opportunity for the Catholic Church to rub it in to that most Protestant institution, established by Queen Elizabeth in 1592.

Anyway, I agreed to write and do a reading at the Youth Mass during the papal visit, which was to take place on Sunday morning in Ballybrit Racecourse just outside Galway city. And I am glad I did.

I had to miss the ceremonies in the Phoenix Park in order to head to Galway. I did most of the journey by car but didn't realise I was going to have to hike through the night for the last six miles of the journey.

While the Pope and his entourage were safely asleep in the Papal Nuncio's residence on the Navan Road, the twenty-three-year-old student activist from Ballyfermot was trudging in total darkness from a marquee where we had assembled at 9 o'clock on the Saturday night for a morale-boosting session.

Young priests like Father John Wall and Arthur O'Neill were unrelenting in their efforts to get us there on time. At 2 AM Vatican time, we headed off on the long march across the fields of Galway. Thousands of young people marching towards a racecourse in the middle of the night, up hill and down dale, across fairy forts, tramping over every pagan memorial ever built!

Sunday dawned over Ballybrit cold and foggy as we crested the hill above the racecourse. The size of the crowd that greeted us below was overwhelming – and indeed was to me the highlight of the day. Outpourings of joy and great fervour were the order of the day.

Every utterance of Pope John Paul was greeted with tumultuous applause. And when the great man from Poland uttered the immortal – but slightly meaningless – phrase 'Young people of Ireland I love you', the whole country collapsed into paroxysms of gratitude and hysteria.

I was ushered onto the altar to utter my few words about giving our political leaders the good grace to act justly. Looking around at the other three people on the altar: the Pope, Bishop Eamonn Casey and Father Michael Cleary, we must have made a pretty picture.

It was a great day, a great time. Little did I know that it would be a watershed in the history of the Catholic Church, marked most noticeably by the personal fortunes of the two other people who stood alongside the Pope and myself on the altar that September Sunday in 1979: Bishop Eamonn Casey and Father Michael Cleary.

JOE DUFFY is the presenter of *LiveLine* on RTÉ Radio 1

Mobile phones in workroom
Key of front door Ted?
evenings dinners 1 person + Sara
phone calls not told hysterically funny.
voting card It was awsome - 35 1⅓ m people s Park ⅓ v pop
This guy

'Dublin was like a deserted city'

The Pope arrived in Ireland at the tail end of my teenage rebellion against pretty much everything he stood for, which to my mind at the time was contraception, a dated attitude to divorce, boring Masses, piety, First Fridays and vague mumbles of contrition, mostly in Latin. I had him pictured in my mind as so much a part of times gone by that I half-expected him to arrive with an armada off Wexford.

I had at this point long since established myself as a bit of a religious rebel. I had already taken my parents aside for a few words about the whole leaving-the-house-for-an-hour-on-Sunday routine and as a result had been granted a dispensation, meaning I no longer had to pretend I was getting Mass. I became the first of my family not to have to pretend to go – much to the amazement of my elder brother and two sisters.

At school, we had taken the religious debate to the point where, by sixth year, I was being excused class to go instead to the career-guidance teacher's office, where he and I debated God's very existence. This had been adjudged to be too disruptive in the classroom; on days when I couldn't avoid the class, we were reduced to simply reading the Bible aloud, with no questions.

Hence when the big fellah arrived in Ireland, it was a given that there was one boy who wouldn't be visiting his local park that day. It was all the more galling for those who would have preferred me to go that I could actually see the Papal Cross from my bedroom window in Drimnagh. 'He came that far for you,' they'd say, 'but you won't walk down the road for him.'

But on the day, I *did* walk down the road, in a way. My best friend came over to the house and we listened to records and made plans to form a band. Later in the afternoon, we walked down to his house in Kilmainham. Dublin was like a deserted city. There were no cars or buses and almost no people. It was so quiet we stopped at a zebra cross-ing to try and re-create the sleeve of the Beatles' *Abbey Road*. I took off my shoes but we really needed two more people.

All the time, the backdrop to our shenanigans was a faint mumbling coming from the Park – a rumble of mumbling, as it were. We had a great day, savouring the rebellious independence of simply not doing what it appeared that everybody else in Ireland was doing.

It's only with hindsight that I can appreciate what a pivotal time it was in my life. I had little understanding then of what a great man John Paul II was and is. He would inspire me now in ways I was then too immature to see. At that time in my life, the Catholic Church spoke to me only of a time that was past. It was as if Ireland was still in the fifties and the rest of the world and my generation were rushing towards a bright and exciting future.

I didn't want to waste time with the Church. Ahead of me lay college and an opportunity to immerse myself in the company of my own generation. When I started later that year, the conversation wasn't of the Pope's visit. It was of bands, of punk, of banned films and books, of being able to get served in the student bar, and of being able to buy condoms in the student union. Formation praying didn't get a look-in.

TOM DUNNE is the presenter of *Pet Sounds* on Today FM

'MY EDITOR HAD HIS EIGHT HUNDRED WORDS

ON TIME'

The Pope's visit was both the most spectacular effusion of Irish piety of all time, surpassing even the Eucharistic Congress in 1932, and the biggest Irish party of all time.

We all know that three and a half million people – in other words, practically everybody – took to the streets over those three days, but what were they all doing there? As always, the motives underlying people's behaviour were mixed: there was a great deal of joy at the visit, and real Catholic reverence, but at the same time hundreds of thousands of Irish men, women and children were simply determined to have a good time.

My job was to cover the trip for the *Sunday Independent*, the *Irish Independent* and the *Evening Herald*, along with dozens of other journalists, many of them far more eminent than I was. So, for me, the visit was round-the-clock work servicing a morning, evening and Sunday newspaper, and a lot of travelling around Ireland in between.

Probably because of my natural scepticism, I found I didn't share in the apparent euphoria as fully as I would have liked to. This made it difficult for me to reach into my heart and find the words to describe what was, indeed, a truly remarkable few days.

On the Saturday, with instructions from *Evening Herald* editor Vincent Doyle to file eight hundred words of colour by noon from the Phoenix Park, I found myself utterly without inspiration as I sat in a vast tent with hundreds of other journalists. Then my wandering mind tuned into one of the dozens of television sets in the tent and I picked up the sonorous words of Brian Farrell intoning, with a seemingly effortless grasp of the liturgy, on the subject of the Pope's first hours in Ireland. Farrell's brilliant account gave me the language I was seeking and, with no apologies for plagiarism, Mr Doyle had his eight hundred words on time.

The following day, at Knock, I had the consolation of observing the great John Healy of the *Irish Times* in a similar dilemma. John, searching for the words to describe the enormity of the day when the Pope had set foot in Healy's native Mayo, sat at his typewriter for about four hours sweating profusely, without a sentence coming out. Eventually, as happens with all journalists, the imminence of the deadline kick-started him, and he launched his typewriter into life at about 7 PM, to finish filing two hours later.

Perhaps the most bizarre sideshow of the entire visit was the spate of rumours flying around among the hundreds of journalists about the President of Ireland, Dr Patrick Hillery. It was rumoured that his marriage to Dr Maeve Hillery was in difficulty and that stories were about to be published in the *Daily Mail* and other newspapers.

I saw a young British journalist standing at one of the banks of telephones at Shannon Airport, clearly under pressure from her news desk to ask the President about the rumours. An hour later, after the Pope's plane had just taken off, I saw her slip up beside the President to ask the fateful question. Dr Hillery visibly stiffened and walked away from her, but the panic engendered by the rumours prompted him to call an ill-advised press conference in Dublin a couple of days later to deny the speculation about his marriage.

We journalists seemed to spend a lot of time waiting around, very often in large tents, with nothing much happening. We also rattled around Ireland in the middle of the night on specially provided ghost trains which swept through empty stations in the small hours of the morning, full to the gills with journalists, quite a few of whom took the time-honoured method of relieving boredom: making sure they had plenty of beer in their carriages.

But it wasn't always about Guinness either. I recall two Cork journalists, Val Dorgan and T. P. O'Mahony, both of whom liked nothing more than a pint, being offered a phial of Valium by a well-known London-based journalist. They were horrified, and rejected the offer – which had been kindly made – with some indignation.

When I met the Pope in Rome a few years later, I reminded him of his Irish trip. His eyes lit up and he became greatly animated. *'Irelande, Irelande!'* he exclaimed. 'Thank you, thank you!'

Ah yes, for believer or sceptic, the welcome the Pope received was a tremendous expression of love for a man of remarkable stature who bestrode the last quarter of the twentieth century as nobody else.

To Pope John Paul II, I would humbly say: 'Thank you, thank you!'

AENGUS FANNING is the editor of the *Sunday Independent*

'A REMARKABLE DAY FOR ALL OF US'

Joan and I flew back via London from somewhere – I can't now remember where – for the Pope's visit. As we checked in with Aer Lingus at London Airport, Frank Pakenham – Lord Longford – arrived, together with a young woman journalist who had been interviewing him on his way to the airport by Tube. I had known him for almost half a century, since he had visited our house in 1933 in the course of undertaking research for his book *Peace by Ordeal*, on the 1921 Anglo-Irish Treaty. As my father had walked him up and down our avenue – in what turned out to be a vain endeavour to convince him that de Valera had behaved badly over the Treaty – I, a seven-year-old, had driven beside them in my little pedal car.

At the Aer Lingus check-in desk, Frank was carrying a folding chair, and he enquired anxiously of me whether I thought there would be room for it at the Pope's Mass in Knock. Wishing to reassure him, and concerned not to shake his evident faith in my omniscience, I eyed the chair professionally, tried to look as if I was engaged in a complex calculation, and then opined that there would probably be ten square feet per person at Knock, which should be sufficient for his chair. He seemed quite relieved to receive such a considered and apparently authoritative reassurance.

Next day, Joan and I were driven to the Phoenix Park for the Pope's Mass, bringing with us her eighty-two-year-old aunt and godmother, Emily Brenan, the only surviving member of her mother's generation. There we were seated near the front, across the 'aisle' from the government, on a bench reserved for the Council of State. Emily found herself beside Siobhan McKenna, who was accompanied by her sister.

At some stage during the Mass I found I had to go the VIP lavatory, which was behind the altar. This entailed an embarrassing walk across in front of the government. While in the lavatory, I was told by someone of a malicious and false story that had been circulated that day about President Hillery. The story was later attributed – I don't know with what, if any, foundation – to a political move within Fianna Fáil to force him to resign the Presidency.

When John Paul II was driven away in his Popemobile at the end of the Mass, Emily Brenan, who was a very religious woman, took out her cigarette machine, rolled herself a cigarette, lit up and, turning to Siobhan McKenna, remarked: 'I don't know what you would call that, Miss McKenna, but I would describe it as a great religious hooly!' Siobhan semed impressed with this summing-up of the occasion.

Later that day, Joan and I were driven to the Nunciature in Cabra, where the Pope was to meet the leaders of our state. We were put into a very small room, together with Frank Cluskey, leader of the Labour Party, with whom we were very friendly, and whose wife Eileen had died some time previously.

I suddenly remembered that I had meant to say to Jack Lynch that he should take this opportunity to raise with the Pope the Church's positon on mixed marriages, which in the Irish case had made a major contribution to the decline of almost 50 percent in the Protestant population of our state during the previous half-century. This decline had been used in Northern Ireland by fundamentalists like Ian Paisley to stir up bigotry, by falsely alleging that this population decrease showed that, since independence, Irish governments had been persecuting Protestants. Two and a half years earlier, as foreign minister, I had myself raised the issue of mixed marriages in the Vatican with both Cardinal Casaroli and Pope Paul VI, but had received a negative reaction. I felt that perhaps this new pontiff might be more open to such a representation.

As the Pope was running late, I decided there would be time to go across the corridor to a large room where Jack Lynch and his government were waiting to speak to him about this matter. Jack's response to my query was to say that President Hillery had wanted to raise the issue when the two men had met the Pope earlier in Áras an Uachtaráin but that, because the Pope was late and rushing, he had been unable to do so. He, Jack Lynch, would try to take it up with the Pope if time permitted during his visit to the Nunciature, and I said I would also try to do so. Only later did I find out that this brief conversation had been televised – fortunately, without sound.

Back in our small room, Joan, who still smoked occasionally, lit up a cigarette, whilst Frank Cluskey found himself a gin and tonic. A knock came at the door. They hastily hid the cigarette and drink behind a curtain as I said 'Come in!' The door opened and a burly priest entered, looked around the room, said 'I'm just casing the joint' and left again. I remarked on what had seemed to me to be a Chicago accent and, recalling a book on American gangsters I had read as child, added 'It could even be from Cicero' – a suburb of Chicago that had been notorious in the 1930s. I later discovered that our visitor had been Monsignor Marcinkus – of whom I had never previously heard – and that he was in fact a native of Cicero!

The Pope's visit to our room was very brief. There was no time to raise anything with him – nor had Jack Lynch had a chance to do so, I heard later. But it had been a remarkable day, spiritually and emotionally, for all of us, both politicians and people. That's why I remember the events of the day so clearly.

GARRET FITZGERALD was Taoiseach from 1981-82 and 1982-87

'THANK YOU FOR YOUR MOST BEAUTIFUL SINGING'

On my return from a holiday in Portugal, I was thrilled and honoured to learn that, at the request of the late Archbishop Ryan, I was invited to sing as a cantor at the great Papal Mass in the Phoenix Park on that historic day in September 1979 when Pope John Paul II delighted Ireland with his presence.

My undying memories of that unique day commenced when my late husband Peter, my son Hugh and I started out from home at the crack of dawn in order to be in good time for the ceremonies. It was impossible not to be caught up in the tremendous joyful excitement as the entire population of Dublin wended its various ways to get to the Park for this wonderful event.

In sequence, my next memory is of singing the beautiful 'Lourdes Magnificat' at the entrance of His Holiness. Then, when he arrived at the high altar, I caught his eye and he smiled at me. The whole Mass was profoundly impressive, and I had the honour of receiving Holy Communion from the hands of Pope John Paul.

When he was leaving, I looked up and saw that His Holiness was walking towards me. To my astonishment, he broke ranks with his security people, came over, shook my hand and thanked me for, in his words, 'your most beautiful singing.' Unfortunately, at this stage the sound was turned off but the television cameras were still rolling, so I have the picture.

Soon afterwards, I was awarded the high papal honour of 'Pro Ecclesia et Pontifice'. I shall remember to my dying day the wonder of this great pontiff's historic visit to the city of Dublin: the sheer joy and happiness that spread like a huge rainbow throughout the vast crowd. It was a heart-stopping experience, never to be equalled.

DR BERNADETTE GREEVY sang as a cantor at the Papal Mass in the Phoenix Park

'THOSE IN RELIGIOUS LIFE HAVE BEEN TOPPLED

FROM THEIR PEDESTALS'

For three days in 1979, normal life was put on hold in Ireland for the visit of Pope John Paul II. Between 29 September and 1 October, two and a half million people flocked to see him, seven thousand Gardaí were detailed to his security, and the media was full of little else. In effect, the Pope mobilised the country, sweeping all before him in triumph.

The newspapers from that period indicate a time of charged emotion. Over a million people gathered in Dublin's Phoenix Park for the first of Pope John Paul's public engagements on Saturday 29 September. They had arrived at dawn and were in a state of great anticipation by the time the Pope's plane, the *St Patrick*, flew overhead. Conor Brady's lyrical report in the *Irish Times* reads like something from Revelations:

> Excitement mounted steadily in the Park, from the moment the *St Patrick* flew into view, coming out of the rising sun in the east with its jet-fighter escort. It flew low over the crowd at 2,500 feet, making a slight roll with its wings as it banked off towards the airport. The huge crowd burst into applause and cheers, a forest of papal flags appeared, and many people wept openly.

Looking back from the vantage point of today, the days of the papal visit have an almost innocent look about them, and the contrast with today couldn't be sharper. The enthusiasm of 1979 appears as an expression of a great, underlying faith which has diminished sharply in the meantime. At least, it must look that way to a lot of people, but I'm not so sure. If there were that many true believers in the population in 1979, why did so many people drift from the Church in the late eighties and early nineties, before the merest whiff of a clerical scandal? It doesn't quite add up.

I speak as someone who was a part of this. My family drove from Dungarvan to Limerick for the last leg of the Pope's visit, setting off in the dark, arriving somewhere miles from the racecourse. Everyone else got there before us – all four hundred thousand of them – and we had to settle for a view of people's backs, as we stood ankle-deep in the mud. In retrospect, I marvel at the force which impelled us to that point. Ten years later, between leaving school and starting college, I went to London. I awoke one morning to realise that I hadn't been to Mass for a month, and I set off in some anxiety to find a Catholic church. I found myself standing among the world's sparsest congregation, and I cringed with embarrassment at it all. I didn't know why I was there, and I was never the same again.

I know I'm not the only person in Ireland with such a story to tell, and indeed I suspect our number is legion. It makes the country's reception of the Pope look rather curious. What was it all about?

Father Martin Tierney was a member of the Dublin organising committee for the papal visit, a man pretty much in the eye of the storm as far as that three-day whirlwind visit was concerned. Talking to him, it becomes clear that Ireland's welcome of Pope John Paul was about a lot more than just religion or faith. It was an expression of our past and our culture, and it had much to do with our perception of the wider world, including what went on in the Vatican:

> For people of my age, the Pope would have been epitomised by the austerity and severity of Pius XII . . . The Pope for most people was an extremely remote person who was locked in the Vatican. Twenty years later, people have become very blasé, as the Pope has been all over the world, but back then, people were absolutely honoured by his visit. It was a time of special blessing.

The visit to Ireland was only the second foreign engagement of John Paul's pontificate, and on top of the novelty factor, there was the deep resonance it held for a country that had suffered for the faith and kept its flame alight when Christianity had faded elsewhere:

> The Pope's visit would have marked the apex of Catholic triumphalism in some senses. Ever for people who were non-churchgoers, Catholicism would've given a national identity up to that time. People would have seen going to Mass on Sundays as no different in some senses, culturally or traditionally, than going to a GAA match in the afternoon. It was part of who you

were and what you did. The Pope's visit tapped into our past, into our traditions for the last hundred years.

Which is not to say that 1979 can be explained away in purely cultural and historical terms, and it would be crass to simplify it as such. For very many people, the Pope's visit sparked a revival of faith, and people who'd been away from the Church for years suddenly returned to the sacraments.

But if you concede that things like Mass attendance and respect for Church hierarchy were fuelled by factors other than spiritual faith, comparisons between 1979 and today become problematic. There's no cultural imperative to practise Catholicism today, and the Catholic Church isn't the only exponent of ideas on the hereafter. Looking at it logically, you'd have to say that anyone who attends Mass now does so out of a conscious choice, a genuine conviction. Whatever about the flocks and shepherds of old, there aren't too many sheep filing into church these days. Martin Tierney agrees:

> My own observation from the people who come on Sundays is that they are there because they want to be there. I detect that in the attention people pay to sermons, they are looking for a preacher who will preach the full Gospel with power. There's a deep, spiritual longing in people and they see the Mass and the sacraments as a way of ritualising that relationship with God. I see that as enormously positive.

Of course, the one glaring difference between 1979 and today is the change in the public's perception of the clergy. Men like Tierney became priests in a time when people queued up to kiss the hand of the newly ordained, so apart were they held from the rest of humanity. Not so any more. The disturbing revelations of recent years have seen those in religious life in Ireland well and truly toppled from their pedestals. Insofar as the focus of devotion has shifted from the Church to the Almighty, Father Tierney doesn't mourn the loss of status:

> I think, in a sense, in the past, the Church was almost an obstacle, and the institution became more important than the God it was meant to facilitate us to know and love. Nowadays people are able to make the distinction between religion and

91

spirituality. Those who go to Mass now, their faith is much more personal in that they see it as a relationship with the God who loves them. The Church would be less important, what it says or what it does.

And it's for that reason more than others that the events of those heady, autumnal days of 1979 are likely to remain unrepeatable. Never again will this country convulse as one for any leader, religious or temporal, and whether you want to see that as loss or change, it's only a question of a point of view.

MARK HARKIN is a Dublin-based journalist who was a magazine editor at the Jesuit Communication Centre between 1998 and 2002

At the time, I was Detective Inspector at the Special Detective Unit in Harcourt Square, Dublin. Along with Detective Superintendent Hubert Reynolds of Garda Headquarters in the Phoenix Park, I was detailed to travel on the papal flight to Ireland. Our role was general security on the flight, liaising with papal security, checking members of the press and issuing accreditation cards to each of the two hundred and forty reporters on board.

On the outward journey, we met Captain Tommy Farrell, who was retiring, and who was extremely proud to be chosen to pilot His Holiness to Ireland. No difficulties were encountered and we took off from Rome on schedule for Ireland, with the Pope on board. During the flight, Father McGee entered the main cabin and informed the press that His Holiness the Pope had agreed to talk to them. The plan was that Pope John Paul would walk down one aisle, around the back and up the far side. However, this was on the condition that 'all concerned would remain in their seats.' Everyone appeared to accept this, and within a few minutes the Pope appeared. Immediately, the main body of the press rose to their feet and surged towards His Holiness. This caused the 747 to dip forward, but in the excitement of the papal presence, this fact appeared to pass almost unnoticed.

As the Pope made his way down the aisle, many of the press, including some of those who had already been spoken to by him, rushed to the back of the plane, some climbing seats seeking another interview. In one case, the Pope replied: 'My good man, haven't I spoken to you only a short time ago?' and ignored the question. The Pope's aide was less considerate as he passed the reporter.

It was common knowledge that the Pope liked to consume a big breakfast and did not eat again until late evening. He was reported to say that he really enjoyed the breakfast on the flight to Dublin, and in particular the black pudding. This was reported in the USA, and consequently the same breakfast was included on many US menus for St Patrick's Day. Aer Lingus's catering division got a large order, especially for black pudding.

As the plane passed over Dublin, someone pointed out that we were flying over the Phoenix Park. I could see crowds of people converging on the central point: the altar. Suddenly, everybody stopped, and in the same instant they looked up and waved wildly. This was a most touching and memorable moment for all of us watching from the plane.

I was in the presence of the Pope in the Phoenix Park, and at Dublin Airport on his return from Knock Shrine. I have spent a great deal of time in my Garda career involved in the arrangements for security and protection for VIPs and heads of state. One of my first duties as a young detective was protection at the Kennedy home in Dunganstown, County Wexford, during the visit of President John F. Kennedy, when I was close to the President. While I value those memories, the real highlight of my career was the privilege of flying with the Pope to Ireland. It was an exceptional experience to feel the charisma of His Holiness John Paul II.

MYLES HAWKSHAW was the detective on the plane that brought the Pope to Ireland

'POPE JOHN PAUL CAME TO IRELAND IN JESUS' NAME'

In 1979, I was stationed at our house, Blessed Sacrament Community, in Cleveland, Ohio. I recall accounts of Pope John Paul II's visit to Ireland. His visit to Mary's Shrine in Knock, County Mayo. The huge crowds in Limerick, and the vast numbers of people for his visit to the Phoenix Park in Dublin. The faith of the Irish people. His Holiness wished to go to Northern Ireland, but there were obstacles to him going there. He was afraid of certain attitudes, and of violence. His Holiness being a man of peace and reconciliation, the virtue of prudence prevailed. Pope John Paul had come to Ireland in Jesus' name! Coming as pastor and leader, sharing his love for his people. Here he reached out to the whole world – the youth, families and leaders – calling them to follow Jesus and live the Christian life.

My mind goes back to Mark 3, where Jesus is speaking to the people – ordinary working people. He was tired, and a person in the crowd came and told Him that His mother was there to see Him. He looked around and asked: 'Who is my mother?' Looking around again, Jesus said to the crowd: 'Here are my mothers and my brothers.' He continued: 'Whoever does God's will is my brother, sister and mother, Brothers and Sisters of Jesus.' Love of Jesus and His people prompted Pope John Paul II to visit Ireland to promote his message of peace and justice.

BROTHER MARTIN HAYES SSS lives in Cleveland, Ohio

'HOLY FATHER, I HEARD YOU WERE
A GREAT GOALKEEPER'

The Holy Father was hardly aware of it but twenty-five years ago he caused me considerable trauma.

It all began in a famous tavern, Mulligan's in Poolbeg Street in Dublin.

As usual, I was sitting in a neutral corner assiduously minding my own business.

I was aware that the Papal visit was imminent but didn't expect that it might impinge on me.

In came Vincent Jennings, who was then Editor of the *Sunday Press*.

I was mildly surprised; he wasn't often seen in that venerable public house.

I became alarmed as he approached me as the crow flies.

When the usual observations about the weather and the state of the country had been exchanged, he looked me straight in the eyes.

He said – and I quote: 'You will cover the Papal visit for me.'

You could have knocked me over with a cliché.

Eventually I recovered and said: 'If you can get clearance from Sean Ward.'

Sean was the Editor of the *Evening Press,* the paper to which I was attached. Vincent went on to detail my brief. I would be on the front page every Sunday and would do a diary for the inside pages.

Now, I had – and have – the greatest respect for the Holy Father but I didn't fancy chronicling his every move.

And I could only hope that Sean Ward would answer Vincent with a resounding 'No.'

Sean was out of the country and I had to sweat for about twenty-four hours before I bounded free.

My respect for the Pope had two sources.

For a start he was a native of Poland, a country not unlike our own.

It is much bigger but has long been subject to hostility from two powerful neighbours, Germany and Russia.

We are between the United States and Britain, which are not hostile but culturally influential.

My second reason for admiring the Pope was that in his student days he had been a goalkeeper.

I have yet to meet a goalkeeper in any game for whom I didn't have a smidgeon of respect.

There was a third reason for my warm feeling towards the Holy Father.

I believed that his accession to the Papacy had been the catalyst for the ferment that liberated Eastern Europe.

He may not have been directly involved but because he was the first Polish Pope there was a whiff of revolution in the air.

Josef Stalin once said: 'How many regiments has the Pope?' It was a crass question.

The spirit will always overcome brute force though on occasions it takes a long time to prevail.

When the Pope travels, as he so often does, he is a symbol of the spirit.

I have vivid memories of his visit to Ireland, especially of the day when he visited the Phoenix Park.

I can still see the streams of people passing through my street in Dublin's South side.

Many were carrying food that would do for several days. Big cider bottles filled with milk were the highest common factor.

I had my own private worry: a friend of mine, a racehorse trainer with no land of his own, used the Park to work his horses.

I feared that the mass of people would damage the gallops. It didn't and my friend is now a famous trainer.

During that visit I decided to see the great man himself and I did so in the Liberties – I think in Thomas Street.

I saw the Holy Father again in rather different circumstances.

The World Cup in Italy and the Islands was coming to a close. I was in Rome for the Final.

On the Sunday morning my friend and colleague, Charlie Stuart, decided to visit St Peter's. We did so and we took a wicked pleasure in seeing many people turned away because they were wearing shorts.

The great square was crowded with people waiting to see the Pope.

He arrived on the balcony on cue and gave his blessing to everyone, even those who were wearing shorts.

A little while before, he had given a private audience to the Republic of Ireland party. They all behaved with extreme politeness, except Mick Byrne, our physio, a man famous for always going his own way.

When his turn came, he said: 'Holy Father, I heard you were a great goalkeeper. I suppose you'd no trouble with the crosses.'

CON HOULIHAN is a journalist and the author of, among other books, *More Than a Game: Selected Sporting Essays* and *The Harvest*

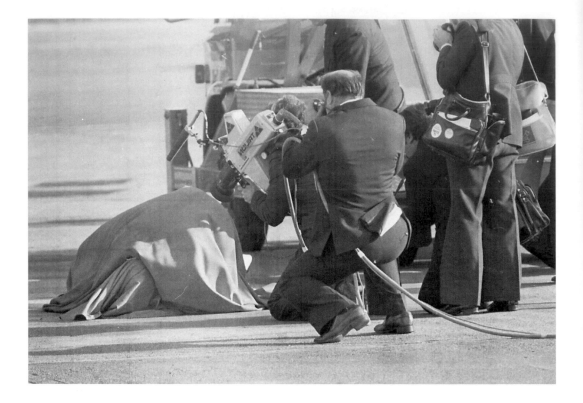

'This guy must be really special'

It was the most important visit in the history of Ireland and there I was, a nine-year-old girl right up there in the middle of the whole thing.

I had been lucky enough to be chosen from a number of children to present the Pope with a bouquet of flowers as he arrived in Dublin Airport. My father, Noel Dromgoole, worked in the airport, and the original plan was to have a group of young children waving flags at the side when the Pope walked down the red carpet. I had no problem doing that job and was not even fazed when my father told me that I had been chosen to present the Pope with flowers. I did not realise at this time what an honour it was or how proud it would make my father.

That Saturday I was taken off to the town for a shopping spree (and it was not even Christmas). I went to an exclusive children's boutique in Wicklow Street called Young Ones, where my mum bought me the most beautiful red-and-black polka-dot dress. It did not end there, either. Down I marched to Clery's, where a beautiful black patent-leather pair of shoes was bought, with the all-important high heels. This guy must be really special for me to get a pair of high-heel shoes!

Twenty-ninth of September 1979: the big day had arrived. I remember being dragged out of my warm bed at five in the morning. What on earth had possessed my parents! I was dressed in my finery and given more kisses and hugs from my nana, who was minding my two brothers, while mam, dad and myself went off to the airport.

When we arrived, I was whisked away from my parents and given the pampering treatment. I was brought down to the hairdresser's and given the fattest ringlets I have every seen in my life. As soon as I got outside the door, I was brushing them out. Pope or no Pope, I was not meeting anyone with ringlets the size of sausages in my hair. Anyway, my mum had done a great job herself.

A short time later – and a little nervous – we stood watching a big plane land on the runway. I always remember wondering why was this guy getting such a big welcome: why all the fuss? As this small man came out of the aeroplane and bent down to kiss the ground, a gust of wind blew his robe over his head. I thought this was the funniest thing I had ever seen.

With a gentle shove, a lovely lady called Eithne pushed myself and Russell (who had also been chosen to present the flowers) down the red carpet. I remember thinking: 'Gosh, all these reporters and television crews – this guy must be really special.' As I approached him, I was unusually calm and felt nothing but happiness. Before me stood a kind, gentle man who placed his hand on my head and asked me 'Do you speak Polish?', to which I replied 'No.' What a funny question for him to ask, I remember thinking. He then bent forward and took my head in his two hands and kissed me on the forehead. My heart was in my mouth and I felt such love for this man who I did not really know. He then pressed something into my hands and turned to speak to Russell. As he was speaking to Russell, I watched him closely. I saw his bright eyes, which shone as each camera flashed, and a smile that was so big and wide. I felt happy and content.

Meanwhile, back at my house, my little brother Brian was completely confused as my nana was kissing and hugging the telly and telling the Pope to bless her. Had everyone gone completely mad?

When I arrived back at the airport, we were interviewed by lots of reporters and TV crews. I remember thinking, I need to see my mam and dad, as I wanted to share with them my experience and also to show them the beautiful rosary beads that the Pope had given me. I saw my dad across the room: to say that he was the proudest man in Ireland was putting it mildly. He had a smile on his face like a Cheshire cat. I handed my dad the rosary beads: to this day he has them displayed in a glass case in his front room. Newspaper cuttings of the event from all over the world are also kept in a 'memories' album. It is a piece of history that I was very lucky to be part of and that I can show my children and grandchildren in years to come.

Although I have not become a nun and am not overly religious, the experience of meeting the Pope is one that I think about regularly and can look back on with fond memories for both myself and all my family. It is true to say, like most of the papers, that that day 'Irish eyes were smiling', and none more than mine on the twenty-ninth of September 1979.

LIZ JACKSON presented flowers to the Pope on his arrival in Ireland

'THIS POPE WAS ON A WORLD TOUR;
THE DUBLIN GIG WAS THE PLACE TO BE'

Fold-up chairs make unlikely relics. Cheap and tacky as they were, they nonetheless symbolised a mad few days.

My friends and I, all in our late teens, were unlikely pilgrims. But in truth, this was no pilgrimage. I brought no crucifix, no beads, no holy water: just a fold-up chair and a bag. I mumbled no prayers on the journey, nor considered any penance or self-sacrifice. I went in the expectation that this would be part protest at the wrongs of the world, part celebration of who we were, and part just great craic.

Like just about everyone else there, I was Catholic by accident of birth but had decided to stay that way. I was no second-class citizen from the North, but I was always keenly aware that I was the son of second-class citizens. And the Pope was coming to Dublin and we were going to be there, just like everyone else, because we were as good as everyone else.

Pope John Paul was an exciting figure then, light-years away from the bulk of his predecessors: half-dead, reclusive Italians with crusty voices. Here was the new Pope: the live-on-TV Pope, the sportsman, the linguist, the political Pope, the campaigning superstar and, above all, the traveller. This Pope was on a world tour, and the Dublin gig was the place to be. I wanted to hear him rage against the big wrongs of the day: Thatcher, the Bomb, imperialism, repression, big business, poverty and the paramilitaries.

My need to be included was important to me. While many in Ireland merely accepted or even bemoaned their Irishness, I protested mine. I raged at the inclination of so many of my Southern friends to denigrate life in the Republic. I felt independence was wasted on them.

I had felt little inclination to go to Galway for the Mass for the Young of Ireland, as that meant accepting the patronising 'youth' tag. I was having none of that. I decided not to head for Drogheda either. Like others, my disappointment at the Pope's decision not the visit the North had soured into annoyance. I was not going to be fobbed off with notions of his visiting the Archdiocese of Armagh from the 'safe' side of the border. Knock? That was for the fanatics and the rosary-whisperers. It had to be Dublin. I had to be part of a million-strong throng in the Park.

The recommendation to bring a fold-up chair seemed odd, even corny, at the time. But I had no idea it would also be emblematic. That chair became a mark. Unlike our fathers, we had not felt a great need to conceal our national identity or our religion. Yet the requirement to walk to Belfast's Central Station with an overnight bag and that fold-up chair meant declaring, in a most visible way, who we were and what we were doing. It was easy to join a march and shout slogans at a rally – that was a safe, phoney radicalism – but this was something else.

I needn't have worried. Chair-carrying Irish Catholics arrived at the station from all directions. Marked men and women every one – but utterly unharmed. It seemed that the morning would be memorable more for the autumn sunshine than for my lone march of silent defiance. Perhaps what I had stood up to was nothing more than my own teenage insecurity.

The Phoenix Park lived up to expectations. The scale of the gathering was awesome: a million people – one-quarter of the population – in one field. The excitement was total, the sense of occasion historic.

A tide of people surged along through Chapelizod in the dark, arms linked and almost in step. Those around us as we strode forward were nameless, but in an odd way they weren't strangers.

We found our allotted place well before 6 AM. I had my first slug of neat Powers whiskey from a bottle offered to me by a man I didn't know. It made my toes open and shut and reduced my voice to a squeak.

I remember the sun rising, huge and red above the mist. There was an eruption of euphoria that morning as the Pope's huge jumbo lumbered overhead, en route to the airport. I can still feel the thrill of it.

I warmed to the Pope's opening line: 'Like Saint Patrick, I too have heard the voice of the Irish calling to me, and so I have come to you, to all of you, in Ireland.'

Yet he never mentioned the Bomb, or repression; he didn't lay into right-wing governments, and he left Thatcher alone. I found him long on the merits of the Eucharistic mystery and disappointingly short on the wrongs of my world.

I listened to his Drogheda sermon on the radio and his mispronounced plea to the paramilitaries to call it off. It wasn't convincing, and I'm not surprised they found him fit to ignore.

I returned to Belfast tired but unchanged, grateful for the Pope's visit yet deflated by the tone and extent of his lecturing. I still hungered for something more radical, challenging, and in tune with my world. Perhaps I still do.

DAN KEENAN is the Northern news editor of the *Irish Times*

'I WAS SO SURPRISED BY THE CHEEK OF HER, I SET OFF'

I happened to be in Dublin house-hunting in the Sutton area at the time of the Pope's visit. My friend Helen's mother was doing a reading at the Mass. I had arranged to meet her and my other friends at the Phoenix Park to enjoy our day.

When I was a little girl, the Eucharistic Congress was held in Ireland, and although I was too young to remember it – I was only two at the time – people talked about it for years afterwards: the honour of such a big event happening in Ireland. For many people, the Pope's visit had the same importance.

I was driving on the north side of Dublin towards the Park when the Gardaí stopped me. They were stopping everyone and told me that I couldn't go any nearer to the Park. There were many cars in Dublin that day, as well as buses full of people coming up from the country, so I had to turn around. I decided to go home and watch it all on television, so as to see Helen's mother.

Driving home, I found myself near the top of O'Connell Street. Even though there had been so many cars in the city, by this time the streets were deserted because everyone was at the Mass, in the Park. As I came near the Rotunda Maternity Hospital, an old woman ran out into the middle of the road, waving a walking stick in the air and shouting 'Stop! Stop!' at me. This came completely out of the blue, so I had to brake suddenly.

I had thought she was sick or had been mugged, but once I stopped, two other women came up out of nowhere and got into the back seat of the car. The old woman prodded me with her walking stick and told me to get back into the car and drive the lot of them to an address far out on the north side. She sat herself down in the front seat, waiting for me to go.

I was so surprised and amused by the cheek of her, I set off. They were all chat, and were very grateful to me. They were very nice, actually. I noticed that one of the other two women was young, and one was holding a tiny baby, a newborn. The woman with the baby started crying.

The baby had been born prematurely and had been in an incubator. When the nurse told her that her baby had gained enough weight for her to be released that day, she tried to contact her husband, but there was no reply at home. She assumed he had taken the other children to see the Pope. Then she tried her other relatives and neighbours, but to no avail. She was so heartbroken, with her new baby ready to go home, she was nearly cursing the Pope.

The woman was in an awful state because her husband didn't know all this – and there weren't any mobile phones then. That day, her mother and sister had come up to visit her in the hospital, but they didn't think that they would be taking the baby home with them. There were no buses or taxis, and there weren't even any other cars – except mine! When you look back at it, it really had been an emergency.

So I brought them home, and they kept asking me to come in, but I told them I had to rush off. The granny put a piece of paper in my hand. I read it back in the car:

Trust Him, when dark thoughts surround you.
Trust Him, when your faith feels small.
Trust Him, when simply to trust him seems the hardest thing of all.

When I eventually arrived home, I rushed to the kitchen, put the kettle on and prepared a tray with all my favourite snacks, including my holy water (Jameson!), carried it to the lounge and, sitting in my comfy chair, put on the TV to catch the show. Within two minutes, I fell asleep and missed everything.

PS I just heard on the news that the Pope may be returning to Ireland in the spring. Better luck next time!!

PHILOMENA LYNOTT is the mother of the late Thin Lizzy star Phil Lynott

'"There's the Pope!" we shouted, proud as a chosen people could be'

The Pope came out of the sky and descended into Ireland on Saturday 29 September 1979. It was a magnificently messianic moment. The heavens had been cleared for it, and the earth brought to a standstill. All airports were closed, so that no man but John Paul could come down from above; all traffic had been banned in Dublin city, so that pilgrims must walk to meet him; all workplaces had been closed, all over the country, that the people might be free to greet he who symbolized spiritual freedom.

No other place in the world had made such arrangements, but no other place in the world identified so strongly with the direct inheritor of the mantle of Jesus Christ. 'The Pope is infallible when he defines a doctrine, concerning faith or morals, to be held by the whole Church.' These are the words that echo and re-echo, unbidden to the mind, when all other words, learned off by heart, have faded away. Their meaning is awesome. The Pope knows what God thinks, and says what God means, and the Pope is absolutely right. When the Pope speaks, God is speaking.

The Pope, when we were first taught those words, was a figure unreal as the man in the moon. He lived far, far away. We would never meet him, nor did we expect to meet him, no more than we ever expected to meet God on this earth.

Then a man landed on the moon. And going to Rome was as common – more common, given the cost of a holiday in the west – than going to Killarney. But still the aura of magic remained.

Men might go to the moon, and all of us might go to Italy, but the Pope would remain immobile and unmoved, there in the Vatican, deep in the panting heart of Rome. Also, an Irishman would never be Pope. So we kept our distance and he kept his, and the godliness of it all was right and proper and seemly.

No wonder the nation came to a halt when he came over here. I mean to say, Jesus, Mary and Joseph, who would have thought it, or wrought to think of it. I was in Blackrock when his plane appeared in

117

the sky, suspended over Howth. As it came drifting closer, hearts stopped with the wonder of it all. 'There's the Pope!' we shouted, laughing and disbelieving, and proud as a chosen people could be.

In the Phoenix Park, a million people gathered, happy and carefree and innocent of evil intent as a bunch of babies. Goodwill and good cheer emanated like sunshine, and the sun did indeed shine from a cloudless sky. The ushers and orderlies and security men were redundant. A joyfully corralled nation behaved as if blessed, and thought itself blessed, and *was* blessed when he stood atop his Popemobile and was driven up and down and through our serried ranks, so that no one was far from him, and the Irish people felt as close to God as it was possible to be.

He looked the part: handsome, virile, gentle, happy and gorgeously dressed, in white silk, satin and glowing gems. We never heard a word he said, but no matter, for the words had been with us since birth, and the ritual of the Mass was an automatic reflex genuflection.

We went home content, we Irish who had seen the Pope, and next day we switched on the television to watch his progress through Limerick, Galway, Knock and Drogheda, and those were the days when the earth turned on its axis and the world as we knew it fell completely apart.

He who was infallible spoke rubbish. Black, he said, was white. Faith fled like snow off a ditch. The Emperor was left with only the clothes he stood in. No one has referred to him since but his words will never be forgotten. John Paul II singlehandedly destroyed the authority of the Roman Catholic Church, which had held unchallenged dominion over the minds and hearts of the Irish nation since Patrick plucked the shamrock.

Tu es Petrus
Et super hanc petram
Aedificado ecclesiam meam . . .

'Thou art Peter, and upon this rock I will build my church, and the gates of hell shall not prevail against it. And I will give to you the keys of the kingdom of heaven. Feed my lambs. Feed my sheep.'

This guy blew the sheep off the rock and out of the water.

Women, he said in Limerick, should return to the kitchen sink. Paid work outside the home was bad for them, for their offspring and for their husbands. Contraception was no good either. This was the equivalent of telling children they shouldn't have pocket money or buy Smarties. Shortly afterwards, Mr Limerick himself, Dessie O'Malley, founded a new political party and defined Durex, in the Dáil, as the apex of democracy.

Murder is murder, John Paul declared confidently in Drogheda, looking north, where he had not the nerve to go. 'On bended knee I ask you to stop,' he asked the Provos, and everybody in possession of a telly could see that he was sitting on a chair as he said this, and there was no way, however much the nation still clung to the faint hope that somehow, somewhere, he would show himself infallible, that the viewer could be persuaded that a Pope sitting on a chair was also on bended knee.

Shortly afterwards the people of Fermanagh elected Bobby Sands, Officer Commanding the IRA in Maze Prison, as their Sinn Féin Member of Parliament at Westminster; Kieran Doherty, also of the IRA, was elected TD for Cavan; and Paddy Agnew, also of the IRA, was elected TD for Louth. Cardinal Ó Fiaich's explanation that people saw their elected Sinn Féin representatives as helpful in matters such as gardening – God help me, I'm on the floor laughing as I write this – was seen as so much ecclesiastical shamrock.

The Pope's visit, said Eoghan Harris at the time, would set Ireland back sociologically ten years for about three weeks. He was wrong. John Paul brought us right smack into the twentieth century, and there is every indication that the people are coming of secular age in the twenty-first century. He untied the Gordian knot of church and state and personally exposed the fallacy of infallibility, leaving the holy men in frocks in tatters, for which let us give thanks. God bless the Pope.

NELL MCCAFFERTY is the author of, among other books, *Woman to Blame* and the forthcoming autobiography *Nell*

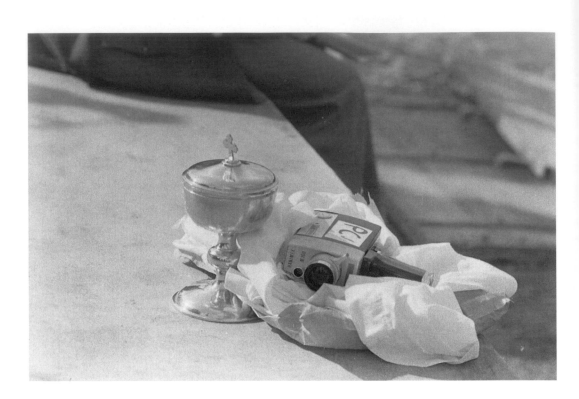

THE TALE OF THE KILLINEER SURPLICE

I suppose that it was the priest's housekeeper who started it all. We were at a meeting on the far side of town when a message came for me to 'do something' urgently. The cattle in the priests' field had broken out and were being chased by the parish priest and the Reverend Mother around the garden, lest they end up on the main road to Dublin. Since they were my animals, I left the function and came to the rescue, armed with a roll of barbed wire, a hammer and a can of staples. As darkness fell, I found myself fencing up the gap, with the aid of the parish priest, and both the cattle and the Reverend Mother had settled down for the night. Naturally enough, I advised the priest about the good and bad points of his sermons, and he strained on the wire while I hammered home the staples. He took it all very well and, a few months later, phoned up to say that he was seeking a good fencer, as a steward at the papal visit to Killineer. Could I come to a meeting in the Lourdes Church on Thursday to receive instructions?

Barney and myself left the Diocese of Meath, crossed the Boyne and heard the plans from Monsignor James Lennon of the Archdiocese of Armagh. Father O'Connor, my fencing assistant, appeared as well, and Drogheda was the scene of unprecedented clerical co-operation. I had known the Pope for some years, as a non-Italian, a rebel with a sense of humour, and a good skier. He had also written a play about love, called *The Jeweller's Shop*. This guy was different, so we were all going to be there. The papal flags were erected at the front gate, and all the stewards were given a yellow and white sash, as a badge of authority.

Saturday the twenty-ninth of September dawned with brilliant sun and I headed off with Barney, leaving Ann at home with four small children, my mother bringing Ruth, while Peter, aged twelve, was travelling with the Tyndalls from up the road. For some strange reason, probably to do with the priests' housekeeper, I was placed in command of a large group of marchers, which included an FCA officer with far more experience of commanding. In the interest of Christianity, he took it all very well.

We gathered beside the Thatch pub at 8 AM and I arrived at Killineer, after a four-mile walk, at 1 PM, armed with a stout umbrella, a picnic bag, and more people than I had ever seen before, even in Croke Park. My role was to keep order around the massed choirs performing at the event. It was a long day, and the helicopter was late, but when the Popemobile came down amidst the crowd, we were closer to a Pope than ever before, and absorbed every word of the famous speech to the men of violence.

When the Pope departed, we set out for home and there was a great mingling. Even the Protestants had come, and were smiling and laughing. Surely things would never be the same again! On the way down the field, I came to a row of pits in the ground with sheets of galvinised covering, which were the septic tanks. There I met Father O'Connor, who had been a concelebrant at the Mass. He was lowering the surplice of his vestments into the pit of stuff, to pull out an unfortunate man who had slipped into the mess. 'Stick to the barbed wire, John!' he called out. I waved – and kept going.

Walking the road to Drogheda was like walking into history; even with weary legs and empty stomachs, we savoured every step. When I met my mother on the road, I knew that she had just spent one of the great days of her seventy-five years. There was a universal glow of contentment. Reaching home at last, I discovered that normal life had continued: Colm, aged two, had fallen out of Grace's wheelbarrow and got a big gash on his head.

The following week, I met Father O'Connor. 'Did you get the surplice cleaned?' I asked him.

'Would you believe, I gave it to a passing local priest who had a similar load for the wash and offered to take it,' he replied.

'Good for him!'

'Not really. It came back in a plastic bag today, as I gave it to him: unwashed!' He continued in a philosophical vein: 'That is one thing I learned from the Pope's visit: to be thankful for a good housekeeper!'

JOHN MCCULLEN has written four books, was a columnist in the *Irish Farmers' Journal* for twenty-five years, and now writes a weekly column in the *Drogheda Independent*

'THE UMBRELLA WAS PASSED REVERENTLY

FROM HAND TO HAND'

Like bookends, the visits to the Republic of Ireland of President John F. Kennedy in 1963, and that of Pope John Paul II in 1979, enclose two volumes of transforming experiences for the Irish people. The Kennedy visit has been analysed exhaustively in television and radio documentaries and in the history books of the 1960s. The three-day tour of Pope John Paul II in September 1979 has been treated as an episode in the life of a Pope who is a global traveller, working to the same formula as that planned for him in the Republic of Ireland. Significantly, the Pope did not visit Northern Ireland in the worsening situation that made Belfast and Armagh unpredictable war zones. Instead, he delivered his best address on the subject of reconciliation and peace in Drogheda.

For those of us who participated whole-heartedly in the first ever visit of a Pope to our shores, it was a blissful occasion. Devoid of begrudgery, we were both host to, and participants in, a succession of feasts. Visually, the spectacular settings of the Phoenix Park in Dublin and medieval Clonmacnoise on the River Shannon were memorable. Glorious choral music, and the sonorous voice of a Pope addressing us on Irish soil, silenced the sceptics and the mockers. In Maynooth, there was the special gift – gratuitously bestowed – of James Galway's hour-long flute concert as the crowds waited for the Pope's delayed helicopter.

Each of us who entered into the spirit of the Pope's visit has a memory of a particular moment. Mine is a story about the Pope and an umbrella. Back in the 1970s, the Irish people were not umbrella users. Put it down to economic reasons (umbrellas were too expensive), climatic factors (it was too windy) or fastidiousness (they were too awkward to carry), umbrellas in the 1970s were black and unwieldy, and not fashion items. This is the context for my story.

On the evening of the visit of Pope John Paul II to Clonmacnoise, I received a telephone message inviting me to join a small group at the front door of Cabra Dominican Convent on the outskirts of Dublin city. Be there at 8.30 PM, I was warned. The Pope was the guest of the

Papal Nuncio, whose residence was in the convent grounds, and the Cabra community offered the Nuncio the facilities of the large convent, in particular a reception hall of handsome proportions for entertaining the Pope's guests, and for press briefings. That particular evening, Pope John Paul II was meeting the Irish Hierarchy privately, so news reporters and cameras were absent. The Pope, I was told, would be driven swiftly up the avenue from the Nuncio's residence to the front door of the convent and would be receptive to being greeted by a small group of people from the locality.

All happened according to plan. Pope John Paul II, at close quarters a handsome, well-proportioned man with an open face, walked swiftly up the shallow steps, pausing to bless a baby held up to him by his mother. There were fewer than fifty people present, women mainly from the housing estates close by, and a few robed Sisters. One slight Monsignor who accompanied the Pope whispered a message to the Sister nearest the door. If we waited until 10.30 PM, the Pope would re-emerge from his meeting, taking the same route. The rain was coming down in a persistent drizzle. Some members of the gathering melted away. One umbrella popped up. We talked in low tones, feeling the chill, and wondered if we too should slip away into the sodden darkness.

Suddenly the door opened and Pope John Paul stood outlined in its frame. As his eyes grew accustomed to the gloom, his glance took in the group huddled around the steps. And then, unexpectedly, he smiled. In a musical, amused tone, he said: 'You should be in your beds!' He was gone into his waiting limousine, the small Monsignor snatching our one umbrella from the same Sister who was nearest the door and had received his original message. In less than two minutes, the Pope had disappeared, but the umbrella was returned, being passed reverently from hand to hand until it reached its owner.

I have often thought about this curious little encounter with the greatest dignitary of the Catholic Church. In a sense, it was a metaphor. That was where women in the Irish Church were in 1979: on the periphery. Inside, on the other side of the convent door, was a great hall, full of light and colour, the scarlet of robes and sashes, the flash of crystal glasses, discreet waiters darting here and there with trays of finger food. Reminded by a kindly Pope of our domestic role, we were patient, docile, invisible, at our best in service roles (useful for supplying an umbrella!). Was our encounter with the Pope a missed opportunity? In the Gospel story there were women uninhibited by place, who spoke their minds to Christ: the scolding Martha; the courageous Mary of Magdala, who went to the empty tomb; the woman who lifted her voice in the crowd and reminded Jesus that He was born of a woman.

If Pope John Paul visits Northern Ireland in 2005 as planned, he and the women of Northern Ireland will have a shared experience of military oppression and loss of family through war. I hope they get the opportunity to speak together. And if it rains, Ireland now has umbrellas large and small for all occasions.

MARGARET MACCURTAIN is a Dominican Sister, a historian and the former chair of the National Archives Advisory Council

'THE SPECTACLE AT GALWAY'

You might say I am a Catholic agnostic. Catholic by cultural background; agnostic through lack of conviction. In 1997, when interviewed for the post as religious-affairs correspondent at the *Irish Times,* I argued that my agnosticism was one reason why I might be suited to the job. Would it be acceptable, I asked, for, say, a political correspondent to be an active member of a political party?

My agnostism was not chosen. It was thrust upon me following aggressive interrogation by myself of my faith in late adolescence and young adulthood. Indeed, it was only in young adulthood that I finally abandoned any idea of becoming a priest, something I had aspired to for most of my life up to then.

This had all happened by the time the Pope visited Ireland in 1979. By then, the only thing I was certain of in this life was uncertainty itself, and I liked to proclaim that the only constant was change – believing the phrase to be as clever as it was true.

My own lack of any real emotional response to the arrival of Pope John Paul in Ireland seemed confirmation that I had passed beyond the strong pull to belief I had struggled with in those many years of wrestling with what I could intellectually accept as true and what I dearly wished to be true.

In childhood I was deeply religious, to the point of being almost neurotic in a scrupulous avoidance of committing even the most venial sin. But my practice was much more positive than this might suggest. I put my Christian beliefs into daily effect, with great seriousness.

As an example: we lived in the countryside of boggy north-west Roscommon for the first ten years of my life. When I was about seven, one Friday in November I cycled the mile and a half to our parish church and saved from Purgatory every relative whose death I knew about and all our dead neighbours in the townland. This I did through separate visits to the church, each visit consisting of the required prayers, etc, to secure the indulgence, and leaving and entering the church for each one as required by Church teaching at the time. Nor was any of this done in a trivial way, but with the utmost conviction that what I was doing was achieving its object. I was a very serious youngster.

I felt very close to God, and prayed regularly each day. It was a very easy relationship. God was my closest friend, not my master. I did not fear him, but trusted him totally, even when I was disappointed that he had not been more co-operative. When that happened, I believed it was for my greater good. I rarely asked for anything for myself.

In adolescence, fissures in my belief began to emerge. These emerged primarily from witnessing how authority was exercised or abused by Church figures locally – by bullying priests and religious Brothers in particular.

I realised that, in conscience, I could never take a vow of obedience which might place me in a position where I would feel forced by such men – acting as my superiors – to do contrary to what I believed was right.

For someone who was seriously considering the priesthood, this was a major issue. Other questions followed: whether Christ was divine, and then the issue of divinity itself.

Up to then, I had been deeply enthused by the documents which emerged from Vatican II, particularly where Church social teaching was concerned. By the time I started attending university, my relationship with God, whose very existence I had now begun to question, was sundering. This was an extremely difficult period. I can only compare it to a bereavement: my first experience of grief.

As though to oblige, God would disappear from my life, leaving an emotional void, then reappear again, only to disappear once more. I had to discipline myself to acknowledge that this was not working for me any more, and I had to accept that fact. I used to joke that God had left me; I had not left God. But I was increasingly coming to the view that neither was the case, but that what I had believed so fervently for so long probably had as little root in truth as Santa Claus and the tooth fairy.

I stopped attending Mass, and endured great guilt for some time. On student working holidays abroad, I would find myself visiting churches, picking up any reading material I could get my hands on, sitting in the silence waiting for . . . something. Rarely did anything happen: there was just an enduring dryness of the soul.

I began to accept that a huge dimension of my life was gone forever and that nothing would, or could, ever fully replace this. It is such real-ization, along with my memory of what it is like to live a life of fully convinced faith, that still causes me greatly to envy genuine people of faith I meet. I don't think they fully realize just how lucky they are.

Yet for me it is no longer possible, if I am to remain true to what I know and have learned about life. For me, the suspension of disbelief – the taking of a leap of faith – would be fraudulent.

I have become what might be called a secular humanist. It means that I feel very much at ease with Christ's second commandment of 'Love thy neighbour.' And I believe that we should cherish the great Judaeo-Christian tradition, with its Greek influence, as probably the most valuable part of our European heritage. Indeed, it prompted what I consider the greatest secular humanist achievement of the last century: the creation in 1946 of the welfare state in Britain.

During those years at college in Galway, I was very much influenced by the existentialist philosophers and some Marxist writers – though I came to believe that Jean-Paul Sartre, for instance, was really not much more than a poseur. I also began to find the extraordinary certainty of orthodox Marxism nothing more than absolute faith by another name. Indeed, I found its certainty about atheism, and atheism generally, to be an extreme expression of faith – albeit faith in nothingness.

The only existentialist for whom I retained any respect was Albert Camus, and that really came down to his humanism. His novel *The Plague* remains for me the quintessential expression of the spirit of Western secular humanism at its most heroic, not least in his character-izations of Dr Bernard Rieus and Father Panelous.

So when John Paul came to Ireland, I was more interested in him as a political than a religious figure. I wondered what impact his arrival on the world stage would have on the future of Poland – little did I antici-pate how hugely influential he would be in the fall of Communism – and how he would deal with the liberation theologians of South and Central America whom I admired so much. And though by then I was considerably alienated from the Church, mainly because of the manner in which it continued to bully though the exercise of an unaccountable authority – not last in the political realm – I also hoped against hope that he might be a Pope in the mould of a (younger) Pope John XXIII.

So I headed out to Ballybrit with a gang of friends. We went out in

133

the early-morning dark, bearing cans of beer, as though we were going to yet another outdoor rock concert. The atmosphere was festive, light, easy, and not at all oppressively 'holy'.

Bishop Eamonn Casey was there: he was someone I admired then as now for the great work he did for so many Irish people in London when no one at home would or could do so. So I cheered him like everyone else. And I cheered Father Michael Cleary because I liked his down-to-earth 'man for the craic' style.

And I met Pat again, one of my favourite friends, with whom I had had a serious falling out – the only one we have ever had – some time before. It was over God. A gang of us went on a camping trip to Clare and in the pub one night we began a discussion about religion, and God in particular. Pat still practised his Catholicism, as did his girlfriend – long since his wife – Eilís. They were among the few of my friends then who still did so.

The conversation in that Clare pub became very heated. A sort of mutual incomprehension engulfed us. It gave way to a belief by each of us that the other was being deliberately provocative and was in fact denigrating the other's position. It wounded. I got angry. He got angry. We dropped it, but I could hardly talk to him for the rest of the night.

We returned to our tents; during the early hours, Eilís came to my tent and asked me to talk to Pat. I agreed to do so. We went for a walk alone in the pitch black, with nothing to be seen but the millions of pinprick stars overhead.

We could hardly see each other, which probably made things easier, as the anger was still there. We couldn't resolve it, and returned to our tents with the consolation that at least we were talking to each other again.

Over time, an uneasy acceptance of each other's position asserted itself in our relationship, which was helped by a shared, ironic sense of humour. In time, our friendship was as strong again as it had been before Clare.

But that morning when I arrived for the Pope's Mass in Ballybrit, Pat looked at me and asked: 'What are *you* doing here?'

Unable to concede an inch, I replied: 'The spectacle . . . '

PATSY MCGARRY is the religious-affairs correspondent of the *Irish Times*

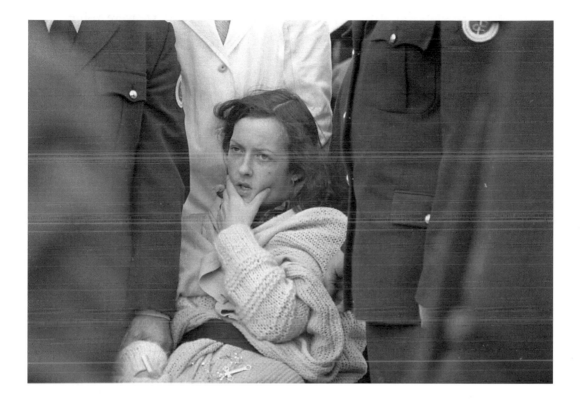

'HIS VISIT CHANGED NOTHING'

We had plans to be out of Dublin that particular weekend. They fell through but, insofar as it was possible, myself and my friends were determined to ignore the visit. It was early days in John Paul II's pontificate, but the signs of his harsh disposition were already apparent. I disliked the way he would rule with an iron fist, and he has done nothing since to change my opinion of him. His performance before the celebrating clerical students of Maynooth College was that of a stern father, listening to their chant of 'He has the whole world in his hands' with a contempt that chilled the heart. Their welcome was violently rejected. And it was captured on camera.

Cameras provided for me also the dominant image of that weekend. At the Youth Mass in Galway, conducting the children of Ireland, in full voice of rapture, were Bishop Eamonn Casey and Father Michael Cleary. If there is ever a moment when the Catholic Church is honest and admits how much it has brought about its own pain, it should look to that day and to those men. The hypocrisy is sickening. Worse crimes were committed than their refusal to acknowledge their kids, but the memory of that jollity defines the weekend of Catholicism triumphant, where ecstatic voices in praise of the Pope drowned out . . . What did they drown out? What ache, what sorrow, what shame, what wound, what abuse? There are many who can answer that better and harder than I can. John Paul II came, he saw and he left. His visit changed nothing. The war in the North raged on. The poverty in the South festered. He did not lessen any suffering.

FRANK MCGUINNESS is a playwright and poet

'THE MOST DOMINANT FIGURE OF THE LAST CENTURY'

In 1933, a small group of Blackrock College students arrived in Rome for a special audience with Pope Pius XI. It was my first time meeting a Pope. Forty-six years later, I welcomed Pope John Paul on board the Aer Lingus 747, *St Patrick*, for his flight to Ireland.

After takeoff we flew at 35,000 feet, passing over Italy, Switzerland, France and England. The Pope sent greetings to the head of each state as we passed. He came up to the flight deck and met the rest of my crew. Pictures were taken by both Aer Lingus and Vatican photographers.

I spoke to the Pope for a short period during the flight. He was very easy to meet, and told me that it was his first flight to Ireland. He gave me a white rosary beads, which I use to this day.

As we approached Dublin, we were met by four Air Corps jets. They approached the *St Patrick* and stayed in formation until almost touchdown. I was particularly pleased with this, as my earlier training had been in the Air Corps.

Flying over Dublin at 1,300 feet, I crossed the Phoenix Park. This gave the Pope a good view of the one million people waiting to greet him.

After thirty-four years in Aer Lingus, this was the most memorable flight of my career. During that time I met and flew many churchmen. The ones I remember most are Pope John Paul and Fulton Sheen.

As I look back over twenty-five years, I feel privileged to have met the most dominant figure of the last century. The visit of the Pope to Ireland was indeed the high point of the history of the Catholic Church in our country. Maybe once again there will be a revival of the faith among our people.

TOM McKEOWN piloted the plane which brought the Pope to Ireland

'A HARD ACT TO FOLLOW'

When the Pope came to Ireland, I stayed in Derry. It was not that I had ceased to be a member of the H, R and C Church or that I had forsaken my allegiance to the man our separated Northern brethren had tended to call 'Old Redsocks'. Karol and I were still buddies; we shared a birthday, 18 May, and the characteristic Taurean characteristics of patience, aesthetic ability and an anger terrible as an army in battle array should our phlegm be seriously upset. (I don't think he actually approves of astrology.) It was just that I had (and still have) a deep-rooted dislike of the public event. I did not relish the prospect of being number 999,998 of the million who would saturate the Phoenix Park or join the dawn trek of Ulster cars heading for County Louth to see the Pope at his most northerly point of penetration. And I was certainly too old to be counted among the 'young people of Ireland' whom he certainly loved.

I did, however, encourage my fifteen-year-old daughter to join her peers in Galway, sleeping in tents and sitting on tiny folding chairs as they waited for the Popemobile to glide past their serried ranks. It was a big moment in her life and she has since had a special care for the charismatic Pole. The visit, it seems to me, was the high point of Irish public Catholicism; the converted were preached to but the appeals for peace went unheeded. (Or, at least, caused the slowest possible germination.) The city of Derry was strangely empty that weekend; there was a palpable sense that its usual population was elsewhere. I went to the 'removal' of a friend's body and the funeral procession was unusually small.

What remains of the visit in flashes of memory are the kissing of the old sod as the pontiff landed, the slightly watchful unease of the clerical reception party, the parade of hired buses seen on television heading south to cross the border at Newry – hardly attacked at all by the 'other side' – and the personality of the man, unmistakably good and Christian, shining through all the smoke and smother. As the Old Irish would have put it: *ní aicde mer,* which in a fairly free translation could read 'a hard act to follow'.

SEAN MCMAHON is an author and editor, and a coeditor of the forth-coming *Brewer's Dictionary of Irish Phrase and Fable*

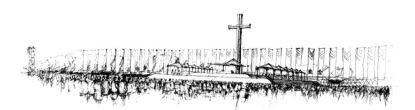

'No Pope here!' I

The visit of Pope John Paul II to Ireland in 1979 made me very angry, for one specific reason. Whoever was in charge of the planning had arranged for him to drop into Clonmacnoise, disturbing some of the holy stones to ease the passage of His Holiness, his Big Bird helicopter lumbering down from heaven onto the hastily constructed landing in the middle of that ancient place. Did no one understand that this beautiful monastic city, on the banks of the broad Shannon, was once one of the centres of the early Irish Church? Our own Celtic church, which had been shorn of its power by Rome's centralising force.

There is a terrible ambiguity here. When the Normans came to Ireland, they had the backing of a Papal Bull, credited to an English Pope, Adrian IV, Nicolas Breakspear. Indeed they came to 'root out' our vices. Before that, we had had our own form of Christianity, with its many delightful centres of worship: those small universities which lit up the Dark Ages. Glendalough, hidden in the Wicklow Mountains; Monasterboice, on the road north through Royal Meath; and other remote, numinous settlements where spiritual meditation was allied with the contemplation of nature at its most wild and beautiful. From this contemplation sprang most of our early art, the glittering illuminated manuscripts, the artefacts like the Cross of Cong and the Ardagh Chalice. And of course the best of our early poetry, with birds singing in the boughs above the bowed head of the busy clerk, and the deer drawing near.

It was as if, with brutal insensitivity, this burly conservative cleric was stomping the hoofprint of Rome onto our defeated church yet again. As if it had never existed as a separate and better-suited way of worship for the devout Irish who had created it. With Colmcille, the Celtic Church had spread into Scotland, the island of Iona, down as far as Lindisfarne: at one historical point it seemed that the early Celtic Church would prevail throughout these islands, and even further afield, in St Gall and other European centres. Toynbee calls it an 'aborted civilisation', and its memory should still persist, and shine for us down the deep well of history.

145

Ironically, the Protestant Church of Ireland has fostered more of this tradition, although our then Cardinal, Tomas Ó Fiaich, was a student of these matters, torn as he always was between his sense of our special destiny as a small, intensely Christian country, and historical necessity. No wonder he looked embarrassed, a bishop of Rome who also came from a source which Rome had helped to destroy, a well it had made brackish. It was as if Pope John Paul were literally trampling on some holy centre of the Greek or Russian or Armenian Orthodox Church, sweeping in his Roman drag through the silence of Mount Athos. I would link this profound insensitivity to his crushing of that wonderful new church which was gathering strength throughout Central and South America and which was a vital response to an increasingly encrusted and retrograde Church of Rome. In fact, the highly conservative Roman Catholic Church under John Paul II was in retreat generally, before the challenges of our times, growing more rigid when it should have espoused real change, as John XXIII had done.

I still almost dance with rage when I think of that pontifical visit to Clonmacnoise, and the arrogant callousness of those who planned it, re-enacting the colonisation of our own once-flourishing church. One of our best poets, Austin Clarke, has evoked the wonders of that early church with its gifted monks and its own holy calendar, all so cruelly smashed by the Invader, with Rome's blessing:

War rattled at us in hammered shirts:
An Englishman had been the Pontiff.
They marched to Mellifont.

Now the former poet and playwright from Krakov was marching to Clonmacnoise, to rub in our loss and defeat on behalf of his opulent Church, as big a business as General Motors. In a spirit of revenge, I relished how the Pope of Rome was foiled in his attempt to cross the Border into our riven North. Surely some way could have been found to bring Dr Paisley's favourite bugbear to Belfast? After all, Paisley himself had gone blazing into Europe to complain about the Pope, 'Auld Red Socks', as he irreverently called him. But no such sense of the absurd leavened His Holiness' visit near the Border. Contemplating the historical irony of the whole visit, I would, for once, have to cry out, along with Ian Paisley: 'No Pope here!' Though on behalf not of Free Presbyterian intransigence, but of the early Irish Church, whose gentle influence was once felt from Clonamcnoise to Iona, before the Church of Rome closed the little monasteries down.

JOHN MONTAGUE's most recent collection of poems is *Drunken Sailor*

'NO POPE HERE!' II

The loyalist prisoners in Crumlin Road Jail cheered and whooped with joy: we were convinced that some Catholics had been killed overnight. We had no radio in our cell but quickly learnt from another republican prisoner that the news had announced the death of Pope John Paul, who had been Pope for just thirty-three days.

The election of his successor, Pope John Paul II, shortly afterwards, coincided with my release from prison and my returning to the editorship of *Republican News* before becoming Sinn Féin's national director of publicity.

Various historical and political repercussions have been attributed to John Paul's papacy, not least that his visit to his homeland, Poland, in 1979, when millions turned out to hear him and got a sense of their real strength, provided the impetus for the Solidarity trade-union movement and the eventual downfall of Communism. It is, however, debatable if he played such a critical role in these events, given that the moribund Communist system couldn't put bread on the table or smiles on the faces of the Polish people.

In mid-July 1979, Cardinal Ó Fiaich announced that the Pope would be visiting Ireland from Saturday 29 September until Monday 1 October. The Holy See said that the details of the visit were yet to be determined and there was great speculation about the reaction of unionists – and possible disturbances if the Pope came north. For northern nationalists, who felt deserted and beleaguered, a visit by the Pope would have been spiritually galvanising and on a par with John Paul's visit to the beleaguered Poles under communist rule.

At the time, I was convinced that neither the British nor the Irish government, nor the Catholic Hierarchy, wanted him to visit the North. Firstly, this was a state whose proud badge was 'No Pope Here'. A visit would have presented a security nightmare, given the likelihood of Ian Paisley-led protests (Paisley had recently topped the poll in the first European elections), the possibility of riots, or worse. Politically, loyalists would have exposed themselves as narrow-minded bigots at a time when the thrust of both British and Irish government propaganda was to hold the Republican Movement responsible for all violence.

If the Pope was to stand on the soil of the Six Counties, how could he remain silent about the reality of life there? On the one hand, he could certainly speak about the ferocity of the IRA campaign. But on the other, if he was to be consistent, he would have to address the violence of the state and thus embarrass the British government. He would have to speak about the torture of those held in interrogation centres, the sectarian loyalist assassination campaign against Catholics for being Catholic as well as nationalist, the situation in the H-Blocks, where men were into their fourth year in naked solitary confinement and suffering ongoing beatings, and the situation in Armagh Prison, where women were locked up twenty-four hours a day and deprived of exercise, visits, letters and toilet facilities. Even Cardinal Ó Fiaich had described the H-Blocks as 'one of the great obstacles to peace in our community'.

On August 27, an IRA bomb killed Lord Mountbatten and three others in Sligo Bay, and a few hours later the IRA killed eighteen British soldiers in two land-mine explosions near Warrenpoint. Even though Mountbatten was killed by the IRA in the South, it was announced that the Pope would not now be visiting the North because of 'the upsurge in IRA attacks'. A Northern visit, which should have been undertaken for pastoral reasons, was cancelled for political reasons.

Two weeks later, there was speculation from sources in Rome that the Pope would make 'a major speech on terrorism and injustice.' Closer to home, Bishop Cathal Daly said that 'the Pope may ask the IRA to put away its guns.' It was easy to see which way the wind was blowing.

There was massive disappointment in the North among the faithful. But people – including many republican supporters – began frantically raising funds and organising buses to go to Drogheda to hear the Pope. I was amazed, and a bit disturbed, at the zealotry. Perhaps if I had been the Catholic I once was, I would have been able to empathise, but I saw only the politics of this visit and expected the play of propaganda and the same things we had been used to hearing before. I remember how deserted our streets were the day he came to Drogheda. I listened to the Pope's speech on television.

Pope John Paul II on his knees begged republicans 'to turn away from the paths of violence and to return to the ways of peace. You may claim to seek justice,' he told us. 'I, too, believe in justice, and seek justice . . . Further violence in Ireland will only drag down to ruin the land you claim to love and the values you claim to cherish.'

I waited for some analysis – however superficial – of the causes of violence, and of the inequalities caused by partition. He referred to Oliver Plunkett's head but not to the people who cut it off. He addressed the politicians. He started off with a token pretence to equivalence of treatment: 'To all who bear political responsibility for the affairs of Ireland, I want to speak with the same urgency and intensity with which I have spoken to the men of violence.' But it was only advice he wanted to give them: 'Do not cause, or condone, or tolerate, conditions which give excuse, or pretext, to men of violence.'

A certain bishop's fingerprints were all over the speech, and an opportunity was squandered to put pressure on the British government to resolve the prison crises and encourage republicans to view an alternative to armed struggle. In June 1981, after the deaths of the first four hunger strikers, including Bobby Sands, Cardinal Ó Fiaich went to the British prime minister, Margaret Thatcher, and appealed to her to make some changes in the prison regime to resolve the hunger strike. She said it would be wrong and dishonourable to give any concessions to the prisoners. Furthermore, she fulsomely quoted the Pope's 1979 speech on 'the men of violence' to justify her position. Subsequently, British governments were to quote Cardinal Cathal Daly's stance in refusing to meet the Sinn Féin president and MP for West Belfast, Gerry Adams, as part-justification for their demonisation of republicans.

'Men of violence' was a phrase coined by Brian Faulkner when he introduced internment in 1971. After direct rule in 1972, it was subsequently used extensively by British secretaries of state and prime ministers. The phrase had pro-British and anti-republican connotations. By no stretch of the imagination was the Pope's use of the phrase simple naivety, or coincidental.

And so, in 1979, despite the Falls curfew, internment, and Bloody Sunday, when thirteen innocent civil-rights marchers were shot dead, the British men of violence were allowed off the hook, were not asked to account for the children, women and men they had killed, for the prisoners they had tortured. Papal excoriation was for one side only: the weaker side, the oppressed. After that, I would never listen to the Pope again, and would never warm to the man.

Yet, an obvious disparity between the Pope's criticism of the IRA and the reality of the wider nature of the war came at the Youth Mass on the Sunday. Two teenage victims of British and loyalist violence were introduced to the Pope. He warmly greeted nineteen-year-old Richard Moore, who was blinded when he was eleven by a British army rubber bullet, and sixteen-year-old Damien Irwin, who lost a leg when loyalists bombed the route of an Easter parade in Belfast in 1977. But the details of these two teenagers and the causes of their suffering were not included in any speeches the Pope made because to have done so would have been to raise questions about the nature of the conflict and why he had condemned only one side.

John Paul II also urged adherence to traditional Catholic moral values and denounced abortion, divorce, contraception, sexual promiscuity and drugs – thus calling into line the changing, and changed, morality of all Irish Catholics. Typically, however, it was his denunciation of the armed struggle which was given most prominence. And so we had discriminating editorials like that in the *Irish Times*, which called on the IRA to say: 'The Pope was right, there is another way', and not the four hundred thousand Irish women on the Pill.

Two days after the Pope left Ireland, loyalist gunmen burst into the home of forty-two-year-old Sadie Larmour, just off the Falls Road, around tea-time, and shot her twice. Her sister and her seventy-eight-year-old mother were also fired on but escaped injury.

Sadie Larmour died fifteen minutes later. When her death was announced on the radio, loyalist prisoners in Crumlin Road Jail cheered and whooped with joy.

DANNY MORRISON is the former Sinn Féin director of communications and author of, among other books, *Then the Walls Came Down: A Prison Journal, All the Dead Voices* and *Rebel Columns*

'THE PAPAL JUMBO JET FLEW LOW OVERHEAD.

VERY LED ZEPPELIN.'

I was eight when the pope played the Phoenix Park. Conventionally enough, my initial memory of that time is of television. There was a *Carry On* movie shown on BBC the night before. The zany theme was something along the lines of 'managing the colonies', uproariously debunking colonialism, Big Ron Atkinson-style, somewhere in Moslem or Hindu Africa or Asia. Hoot hoot! The scene that struck me showed a colonial kid eating a banana (boom . . .) and repeatedly picking his nose (. . . boom!). Something about the nose-picking and banana-eating disturbed to me beyond the sum of the two parts. So much so that I remember describing it to my mother the next day as we disembarked from the free papal bus service through the automatically opening, hydraulically operated centre doors (the old rear-entry black and tans had been replaced by orange-sand upgrades). She told me that picking your nose was indeed a disgusting habit.

The colour-coded papal-bus-ticket crowd-control system that was in effect meant that we ended up in a plywood-fenced area about half a mile from the stage, where we had a picnic and awaited the papal arrival. After an indeterminate time lapse, the papal jumbo jet flew low overhead. Very Led Zeppelin. In my family, we used to come home from visiting our grandmother on Christmas Eve through the Phoenix Park. Our Dad used to tell us to look out for Santa, flying overhead, which we would do feverishly. (He would prep us in November by telling us that the Phoenix Park reindeer herd looked a bit thin: Santa must have picked his team.) So this was a nice permutation of that.

After another indeterminate lapse of time, Il Papa arrived and started into a mega-Mass. I started playing with some other kids until a man reprimanded us for not massing it up like the massed masses massing it up around us. I tried to get into it for a few minutes – I even knelt down and listened – but what was the man thinking? I was eight. The Pope might as well have been talking about hyperbolic calculus or jurisprudence. Thinking about it now, I wonder whether the man was so far removed from childhood that he had forgotten that all a kid can really do is play. What did he think we did: read newspapers, watch the news, orchestrate pretend sermons, form seminal diktat-toting punk groups? I could be sensitive to his point if we were in a church on a Sunday, but it was a sunny Saturday all-day event in the Phoenix Park. All I knew was that Jesus loved us kids and that the Pope probably didn't mind us playing. I drifted back to the bosom of my picnic base, temporarily play-disabled, and started all over again.

After another lapse of time, the Pope drove through the plywood penned-in crowd in his Popemobile, which was the height of technological cool back then. Bulletproof was *it* in the seventies. And then it was all over. I remember being scared of the crowding that occurred coming down off the bluff and out through Chapolized Gate. It wasn't until U2 played Croke Park about six years later that I experienced a crush of more uncomfortable proportions. But then again, the intervening six years can be summed up in one word: school – where there's not much in the way of ecstatic thronging.

A few days later, the departure of the papal jumbo jet was televised. There was something unprecedented about this televised event that I can't remember now: RTÉ being on the air that early in the day, or maybe that it was on RTÉ 2, which would have been another technological novelty back then. I was playing in our next-door neighbours' house and we watched for a while. I can't remember exactly what Mrs McDermott said about the Pope leaving, but I remember feeling sad, whatever it was. She was a nice woman and is dead now.

My Dad didn't attend, instead painting our front door a super-seventies shade of dark brown and ostensibly minding my brother, who would have been about five. I never asked him why he didn't go, but I think that, more than anything else, it wasn't really his style. A few years later, I had to listen to the whole of Self-Aid on the radio, because his nibs wanted to watch every other station on the box. Even *Match of the Day* – and he's from Kilkenny. Anyway, ill wind and all that, I taped a bunch of top stuff that I wouldn't have thought to tape otherwise ('This country belongs to you just as much as it belongs to CIÉ, or AIB, or the Bank of Ireland'), all of which has been sadly misplaced over the years.

I seem to remember my Dad saying that he cried when the radio commentary announced that the Pope had touched down. But my eggshell mind could be a bit cracked on this point. The bird that arrives on the beach of eternity every million years has probably collected more grains of sand than there have been tears shed by the generation of Irishmen born in the 1930s. You can be sure that they got Tears for Fears or the Cure about as much as I got religion in the Park. Maybe he said that he suddenly regretted not going and my kid brain did the rest, processing regret, equals sad, equals crying like a little girl down the misty mists of time. Or maybe the paint fumes got to him.

STEPHEN MURPHY grew up in Dublin but left the country to find work in May 1994; the very next month, the economy took off

'THE CRY OF A PEOPLE BEHAVING ACCORDING TO RULES OF COMMUNITY'

I'm not a Catholic; I haven't been one for many years. I went along to the Phoenix Park to keep my mother company, but anyone who participated in that day participated in something wonderful. It was a truly miraculous day; the spirits of the people were beyond description.

Dublin was extraordinarily well organised, more efficiently governed than at any time in its history. The Catholic Church was then at the height of its glory and power, and everything was arranged superbly.

When the Pope's 747 came over the Park accompanied by the Air Corps, there was a cry that went up from the crowd that was unlike anything I've experienced. It wasn't the cry of a simple, backward people; it was the cry of an intelligent people who were behaving according to some very simple rules of community. It was a transfixing occasion; everyone was bound in unity at that moment. It wasn't a religious occasion in the sense of solemnity, but it was a very religious occasion in the sense the early Christians would have understood.

The next day, I had to go up to the Park to write up the aftermath of the event for the *Irish Times*. The shocking thing was that you could see the progress of the departing crowd by the litter trail that covered the road, about one foot deep. I remember seeing a man in a Mercedes driving along beside all the Portaloos while his children ran into the toilets, stealing the lavatory paper. He cruised along like a Fagin-type figure with the doors open, and the children running backwards and forwards, hurling lavatory rolls in. I suppose that's why he had a Mercedes: he had initiative and nerve.

KEVIN MYERS is an *Irish Times* journalist and the author of the novel *Banks of Green Willow*

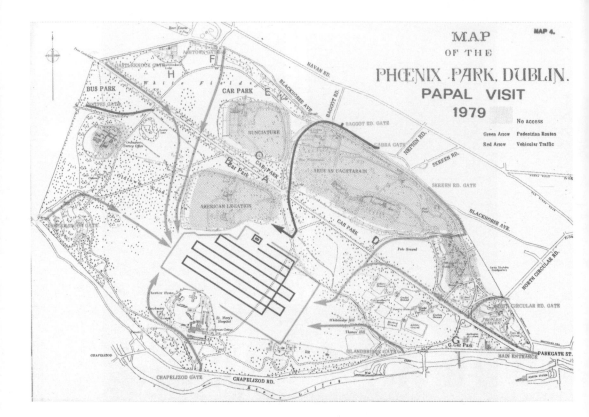

MAP
OF THE
PHŒNIX PARK, DUBLIN.
PAPAL VISIT
1979

No access

Green Arrow   Pedestrian Routes
Red Arrow   Vehicular Traffic

'LOVE ME, DO YA? WELL BLEEDIN' PROVE IT!'

To paraphrase that old routine of Ronnie Drew's: 'Do I remember the Pope's visit? Do I remember, will I ever forget!' I was actually in Sheffield attending a major world conference on gay rights organised by the English group the Campaign for Homosexual Equality and had just completed the presentation of one of three foundation documents that were used in the creation of the International Gay Association when the news came through on the wireless of the election of Cardinal Wojtyla of Poland as Pope. I was elated. I thought to myself: here is an end to the Italian hegemony. What a liberating thing it would be for the Church to have a young, radical, northern European thinker. What a mistake that was. But then I have never been good at guessing the political odds: I even thought, at the beginning of her time in office, that Margaret Thatcher, as Britain's first woman prime minister, would introduce a new regime of tolerance and fairness.

I hadn't completely soured on the Pope at the time of his visit to Dublin: in fact, I was caught up in the whole emotional maelstrom. I didn't have far to go either, because his cavalcade passed right down the bottom of my street, along Sean McDermott Street and Parnell Street. I went down to watch the process buried in the midst of a crowd of oul' wans from the area. I remember the surge of emotion that passed through the crowd as the Popemobile was spotted in the distance. But there was great disappointment that he failed to stop at, or even to gesture towards, the Lady of Lourdes Church, with its shrine of commemoration to Matt Talbot.

The Pope had arrived at Dublin Airport a few hours previously, and as a sardonic friend of mine put it, reversed the usual procedure by getting off the plane, kissing the ground and walking on the women. And then among his celebrated utterances was the heavily accented 'Yonk people of Ireland we loff you.' This brought to mind something I had just heard as I passed a cinema queue in O'Connell Street, where a youth was vainly attempting to canoodle with his mot but was being vigorously repulsed. 'Jaysus, Mary, I bleedin' love ya,' he said. 'Love me, do ya?' she replied. 'Well bleedin' prove it!'

As far as the issue of gay people is concerned, the Pope and his henchman Cardinal Ratzinger have spent the last decades of his papacy demonstrating fairly conclusively that gay people are not included in his otherwise all-encompassing love. In the euphoria of the papal visit, that didn't really seem to register, however.

That weekend, I was working as usual in the disco in the Hirschfeld Centre. The number of young fellas that came fluttering in, their eyes bright with excitement and full of tales of their experience of serving Mass, being altar boys, directing the traffic and so on. I had no idea that the participation of the gay community in the papal visit was so comprehensive. Yes indeed, romances did begin at the Papal Mass, and there are still quite a few long-term gay couples in Ireland who date their anniversary from the Pope's visit. So there must have been something good about it. Just as, in the middle of all the Vatican's homophobia, there is still goodness and decency in the Pope's strong and principled stand on issues such as the war in Iraq. To quote the end line of *Some Like It Hot:* 'Nobody's perfect.'

SENATOR DAVID NORRIS is an author and activist, and a leading authority on James Joyce

'The Trinis slapped their thighs

and fell about laughing'

I'd only come to live in Dublin a couple of months when suddenly John Paul decided he too would come over and check the place out. I'd had a lot of adjusting to do on arrival here; in the first instance, I had to deal with just what to call this state in which I'd decided to live. I found myself saying 'Here . . . in Ireland' rather sheepishly and restraining myself from using the pejorative 'Free State'.

The immediate flurry of activity on foot of the Vatican's confirmation of the Pope's visit flummoxed me. This state was flexing its muscles. The Gardaí were borrowing a helicopter from the former West German police, Irish sailors in uniform were guarding the streets, and the Air Corps were on standby, threatening to down any flying object that came within sight of the plane carrying the Pope. Us northerners ('nordies' had not yet been coined) smiled to ourselves at the notion of the Irish Air Corps, which had never fired a shot in anger, threatening to down intruders in the Pope's airspace.

The day duly arrived, and I made my way to the Park. Of *course* I made my way to the Park: where else would you be on such a day? It was as moving for me as a visit to the Grotto in Lourdes a few years earlier while backpacking round Europe. I couldn't actually see the Pope, such were the crowds, but it was those vast crowds of all of Ireland that rendered the day poignant, filled one with pride, and reminded one of the old saying: 'Once a Catholic, always a Catholic.'

The Chieftains played. I enjoyed that. Very Irish. Paddy Moloney has been recounting the story ever since, covering album sleeves with the information or casually letting drop in interviews that 'We played to the biggest live audience of all time', neatly sidestepping the truth that no one was there to see him or his fellow Chieftains. It was the Pope they'd come for, and between the jigs and the reels, they got to see him.

Later that night, frustrated at not actually having glimpsed the Pope, I wandered unhindered the length of O'Connell Street, awaiting his arrival from Drogheda in the Popemobile. When he did arrive, I ran along the street, paused, raised my arms aloft with a camera in my hands and took a great and dramatic picture of him waving to the multitudes. Nobody said boo to me – certainly no member of the security forces.

As he travelled down towards the bridge, I smiled at the Irish nation's inability to deal linguistically with the presence of the Holy Father in their midst. There was a collective reluctance to shout 'Long live the Pope' or 'Up with the Pope.' (God knows there was no such reluctance to shout 'Down with the Pope' in certain quarters of Belfast). It seemed just too prosaic, vulgar even, in English. And so all the Irish people, exposed to such scenes over the years live from Rome by the miracle of television, wished this Polish pope, the former Bishop of Krakow, well, not in either of their own two languages, but in a borrowed and heavily accented Italian, con brio. 'Viva Il Papa!' they roared.

Ah well. I didn't realise I would see him again, this time close up, just a few years later at Piarco Airport in Port-of-Spain in Trinidad. We arrived at the same time, in separate jumbos. He spoke to those gathered at the airport in the middle of a tropical downpour and endeared himself to the crowd by stretching out his arm and smiling, before pronouncing: 'Nice rain.' The huge crowd of Trinis responded uproariously, slapping their thighs and falling about laughing before launching into a specially rewritten version extempore of Arrow's then-current calypso: 'Raise Yuh Hands If Yuh Love De Pope'. No linguistic shortcomings there.

*

In the years since, I've often wondered what became of the helicopter loaned by the Polizei to the Gardaí. I'm convinced they never gave it back. In fact, I know they didn't, because I saw it in an episode of *Father Ted*, 'The Old Grey Whistle Theft', hovering above the Parochial House on Craggy Island: a neat coda to our wonderful Irish religious *advintures*.

ÉAMONN Ó CATHÁIN is a broadcaster on food and music and the author of *Around Ireland with a Pan: Food, Tales and Recipes*

'The Pontiff appeared, and all hell broke loose'

The Italian press got very excited about Pope John Paul II visiting 'an Irish volcano with many craters,' as *La Stampa* put it. *Corriere della Sera* warned that the Pope was going to an armed camp where Catholics attacked Protestants as heretics and Protestants attacked Catholics as papists. I read these alarmist accounts in Rome during the week before the Pope's first visit to Ireland on 29 September 1979. My brief from the *Irish Times* was to write daily stories leading up to the visit, and then travel with the Pope from Rome to Dublin.

The Vatican press office was as tight-fisted with information as the Kremlin: Donnacha Ó Dualing of RTÉ radio and I spent the days trying to extract information fron any cleric who would talk to us. Father Lambert Greenan, editor of the English-language edition of the Vatican newspaper *Osservatore Romano,* dismissed concerns about the Pope's security in the 'Irish volcano'. 'As far as the Vatican is concerned,' he told us, 'the Pope is more vulnerable here in Rome; if someone wanted to harm him, it would be relatively easy to do so any Sunday in St Peter's Square.' (Father Greenan's words were prophetic: the Pope was unharmed in Ireland but two years later was shot in the square by Mehmet Ali Agca from Turkey.) Nevertheless, the Vatican was so concerned by the blustering of the Reverend Ian Paisley against 'Old Red Socks' that it cancelled plans for the Pope to visit Armagh, the Pontifical See.

Reporters got to see the Pope once before the trip, when he addressed forty thousand pilgrims in St Peter's Square. We spotted a seventy-strong group from St Joseph's parish in Limerick waving tricolours. 'And now,' Donnacha said into his tape recorder as we rushed towards them, 'I see a group of pilgrims from Limerick, waving the flag of the Thirty-two Counties.' (Donnacha was well known for his republican sentiments. In fact, he and the RTÉ producer who accompanied him had confided separately to me that the producer's role in Rome was mainly to exise such sentiments, so I presume the flag comment did not survive the editing process.)

The Pope's last public duty before his tour to Ireland and the United States was to concelebrate Mass in St Peter's Basicila, where one of the arc lights burst with a loud bang as the Pope mounted the altar, causing brief panic among security guards. On the morning of the twenty-ninth, accompanied by his secretary Father John Magee from Newry, County Down, the Pope flew by helicopter to Rome's Fiumicino Airport, where he told a clutch of cardinals and assembled diplomats gathered to wish him safe journey that he hoped his visit would help lessen the tensions that had caused deep division, destruction and death in Ireland.

Aer Lingus, the Irish national airline, had laid on the pride of its fleet, the *St Patrick,* to take the Pope to Dublin. It wasn't such an exclusive deal for me to travel on the same flight as the Pope. Some hundred and seventy members of the media were crammed into the economy section. There was some hilarity after we took off when chief air hostess Catherine Nash announced: 'Holy Father, distinguished visitors, you may now smoke if you wish.' Up in first class, the Pope was engaged in an activity even more dangerous to health: tucking into an Irish fry of bacon, eggs and sausage.

As the *St Patrick* made its stately way through French airspace, the Aer Lingus press officer, Captain Jack Miller, told us that the Holy Father was to pay us a visit. He said the Pope would emerge from the curtained-off forward area, proceed down the left aisle, cross over at the back and return along the other side, so that everyone would have a chance to ask him a question. 'So would you please stay in your seats,' requested Captain Miller sternly.

The pontiff appeared in white coat and skullcap, and all hell broke loose. Some Italian photographers rushed towards him, climbing over rows of seats, stepping on typewriters and shoulder bags. Then we all crused forward, fearful we would miss out. The huge aircraft tilted perceptibly as its human cargo shifted to one side. The pilot quickly righted the 747, two uniformed Gardaí restored some order, and the Pope moved towards the back of the plane. Through a mass of microphones and cameras, I heard the religious-affairs correspondent of the *Dublin Evening Herald,* which had a market of one million potential readers gathering in Dublin, get in his one question: 'Holy Father, will you bless this picture?' The Pope fielded some tougher questions too, though. What did he hope to achieve in Ireland? 'Reconciliation.' Why did he not visit Armagh? 'It is a sadness.' Did he hope to bring peace to

Ireland? 'Peace in Ireland is my constant prayer.' After twenty minutes, he retreated to first class.

The 747 crossed over a corner of England – prompting Queen Elizabeth to send a message of good wishes – and entered Irish airspace east of County Wexford, escorted by four Irish Air Corps jets. In brilliant sunshine, the *St Patrick* swept low over the Phoenix Park – and a vast sea of upturned faces.

In Dublin, the coverage of the visit for the *Irish Times* was taken over by a huge newsroom team, including some of the top names in Irish journalism today: Olivia O'Leary, Maeve Binchy, Caroline Walsh, Conor Brady and Geraldine Kennedy.

I rejoined the *St Patrick* four days later at Dublin Airport to accompany the Pope to Boston. He waved goodbye to President Hillery under a banner saying 'SLÁN AGUS BEANNACHT LEAT, PAPA EOIN POL'. As the plane headed west, he tucked into smoked salmon from Dingle and a Creggan lobster, which he told Aer Lingus chief Atlantic hostess Joan Cammon 'would feed a team'. After an Irish coffee, he fell asleep.

This time he did not come back to greet the media. He told us instead over the public-address system that he was grateful for our presence and 'I bless all of your families and your work and the religious objects you have with you.'

CONOR O'CLERY is the US correspondent of the *Irish Times*

'I DIDN'T AGREED WITH THE CHURCH'S RULINGS'

I was surprised at the number of people I knew who were going to the Phoenix Park to see the Pope. Most of my friends didn't go to Mass on Sundays and many of them were ambivalent about their degree of faith, but they still wanted to see him. To be honest, I couldn't really understand why. To me – despite the images of a modern pontiff who went skiing and wore a watch – he wasn't a particularly relevant person. I didn't believe in papal infallibility, I thought Mass was boring (and that most priests needed lessons in how to write a half-decent sermon), and most of all I believed that organised religion is the antithesis of what faith, love and all of that stuff is supposed to be about. And whether or not the Pope was a decent guy, he was still the head of a church that was more of a business enterprise than anything else. To me, going to see him would have implied that I agreed with the Church's rulings on many issues. And I didn't. In fact, I disagreed profoundly with them. I still do.

Maybe I'm just not good on mass adulation either. I didn't scream in excitement when I went to see my then pop idol Gilbert O'Sullivan in concert, even though all around me girls were going crazy. And I thought the lyrics of Gilbert's songs were a great deal more meaningful than anything the Church had to say. So as far as I was concerned, the Pope had no chance.

Most of my friends said that they were going because it was a once-in-a-lifetime opportunity and they wanted to say they'd seen him. Since then, travel has become so inexpensive that you can hop to Rome for a weekend and see him there if you really want, as well as having a wonderful break at the same time. The Phoenix Park doesn't have quite the same appeal!

The truth is that I don't remember very much about his visit at all, other than the fact that when he said 'Young people of Ireland, I love you', I was a young person but I didn't feel particularly loved by either the Church or the Pope. The day he was at the Phoenix Park I went out for a Chinese meal with my partner. The fact that we're still together today is more relevant to me than three days in September twenty-five years ago.

SHEILA O'FLANAGAN's most recent novel is *Anyone But Him*

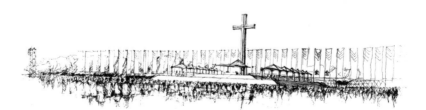

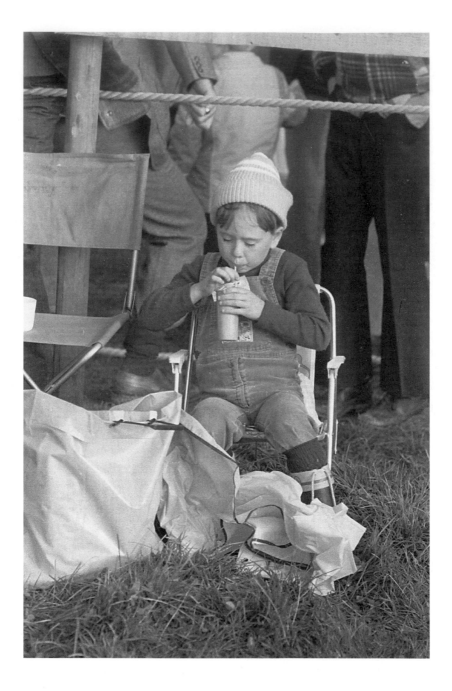

'A MIXED BLESSING, BUT A BLESSING ALL THE SAME'

At the outset, a few disclaimers. First, I am not, generally speaking, a Catholic. I was baptised into the Roman Church but was subsequently brought up squarely in the sometimes warm embrace of the Church of England. Then, to add insult to injury, as it were, around the time I reached adolescence I sloughed off my hitherto strongly held religious beliefs once and for all (or so it seems to me now). Second, I am not, strictly speaking, Irish. I am the product of an English mother and an Irish father, though having lived here for the last ten years gives me some claim to call the place my own. Spiritually speaking, I would probably feel most at home in some neutral land mass in the middle of the Irish Sea (although I don't know whether the Isle of Man would prove particularly congenial). Third, not only was I not in Ireland at the time of the Pope's visit, I didn't even watch the events on television. (We didn't have one at the time.)

For English people, those years were coloured by two national events that fall neatly on either side of the papal visit. In 1977, we loyal subjects celebrated the Silver Jubilee of Her Majesty Queen Elizabeth II. There were monumental street parties, and no doubt lashings of spam and ginger beer as well, though the memory of a six-year-old boy is somewhat hazy on such details. I took the opportunity of dressing up in full Red Indian garb (the phrase 'American Indian' was not then even a twinkle in a revisionist historian's eye), stripped to the waist, 'tattooed' in body-marking crayon with buffalo and other fierce creatures, and equipped with a bow taller than myself to ward off any republican (English, Irish or otherwise) or other arrant knave who might threaten the life of the Queen, should she decide to pay a visit to any of her subjects in our more obscure south London suburb. Then, in 1981, in the depths of a recession, we celebrated the fairy-tale wedding of the dashing Prince Charles and the beautiful Princess Diana. There were not so many street parties this time, as I recall, but still, much celebrating, and wall-to-wall coverage of the event on all the television channels. Commemorative mugs and other paraphernalia were also much in evidence.

Historians may look back on the Pope's visit to Ireland in 1979 as the high-water mark of the Catholic Church in Ireland. With hindsight, both the Silver Jubilee and the royal wedding could be said, when taken together, to mark a high point in a certain type of Englishness: of national self-confidence and belief that the English would, as ever, finish on the winning team. Or perhaps, more accurately, it was a last hurrah for the days of Empire, for the Dunkirk spirit and even for the ideals of self-sufficiency and community that spurred us to 'dig for victory' and then, having (with US assistance, it must be said) defeated Hitler, to set up the world's first Welfare State. Certainly there was far less pomp and circumstance surrounding the Queen's recent Golden Jubilee, which, you might have assumed, would be twice as popular as the Silver. No, the world has moved on apace: the Empire is no more than a few scattered rocks in various oceans around the world, and we no longer believe in fairy tales, at least not when it comes to marriages involving the royals.

*

I was dimly aware of the papal visit, but south London was well insulated, culturally, from the possible depredations of marauding Catholics: Guy Fawkes is still burnt in effigy in even the more tolerant parts of the country. My feelings towards the Pope, as towards the Catholic Church in general – and all churches, for that matter – is that he, and it, is a mixed blessing.

On the one hand, few movements can have left such a trail of blood and bitterness behind them as the Catholic Church has over the course of its long history. And on homosexuality, contraception and other of the hard facts of life, the Pope – or, in the most generous analysis, his key lieutenants – is whistling in the wind. Fortunately, as with Britain and its Empire, the Catholic Church's iron grip over the minds of its congregants around the world has been loosening rapidly in recent years.

On the other hand, few movements can claim to have been such a force for stability, peace and justice in the world as the Church. In the Dark Ages, the Celtic Church and its offshoots kept the flame of learning alive and persuaded warring tribes to live according to the rule of law rather than the dictates of might is right and devil take the hind-most. And in the much-maligned Middle Ages, the pan-European Church to a great extent held society together by giving people of all ranks a clear picture of their position in the world and a commonly held view of the cosmos and humanity's place within it.

In recent times, the Pope's has been one of the few voices (along with those of Bono and Bob Geldof, those quintessentially Irish-middle-class rabble-rousers) raised in continual opposition to the concept that people's energies should be directed exclusively at the pursuit of eco-nomic advantage (which, in many if not all cases, must mean economic disadvantage for others) and, more pertinently, to the madness of war. John Paul II has stated, absolutely rightly, that there is no room for equivocation on this point: violence as a means of resolving conflict is at best misguided and at worst heinous. His words on this matter in 1979 to those who took up the sword in the North are of a piece with his frail yet powerful words to President Bush and Prime Minister Blair on the continuing war in Iraq. All women and men of conscience (and that is all of us) would be well advised to rally behind him on this, if on noth-ing else, as behind a shield while a hail of arrows falls among us. I, for one, will remember with gratitude the Pope's brave and principled utterances on the illegal war in Iraq when I have forgotten almost every-thing else about his pontificate.

If the history of every civilisation that has gone before us is any guide, there is no escaping the life of the spirit. We have a choice, metaphorically speaking, between the psychiatrist's couch and the Confession box. That being so, and after due consideration, I would rather the tarnished beauty of the Catholic Church than the warm but empty embrace of psychoanalysis.

The Church, and its *capo* the Pope, is a mixed blessing certainly but, on balance, a blessing all the same. We would be wise to take them where we find them in these unquiet times.

SEÁN WILLIAM O'KEEFFE is a poet, historian and nervously expectant father

179

'Guys, he ain't talkin''

Even now, the sense of burgeoning anticipation I experienced as the Aer Lingus jumbo touched down at Dublin Airport remains vivid for me. But even as I recall it, I still find it difficult to believe that it all happened twenty-five years ago. The enthusiasm for the visit – the first ever by a Pope to Ireland – was widespread and genuine. The expectations of the event, on the other hand, were exaggerated to the point of being unreal and unrealizable.

In the main, the expectations were two-fold: (a) the belief or hope on the part of the Catholic bishops that the visit of John Paul II would provide some sort of spiritual stimulus, would spark a kind of religious regeneration, a renaissance or renewal of Irish Catholicism, and (b) that the visit would bring about the cessation of IRA violence in the North.

The latter was doomed to failure. In fact, the blunt rejection by the Provos of the Pope's passionate plea at Drogheda – his famous 'On my knees I beg you' speech – became a kind of metaphor for the visit itself. For it too was doomed to failure.

Where now is there any discernible trace of the impact of the Pope's visit? Where now is there any evidence of a lasting effect? Any of us would be hard pressed to come up with a convincing answer, save perhaps in relation to the highly contentious and divisive abortion question.

In the Pope's final speech at Limerick Racecourse before departing for the United States, he issued a rallying call urging Irish Catholics to hold the line on contraception, divorce and abortion. That line has been well and truly breached on the first two issues, and partially breached on the third.

The truth is that the papal visit made no lasting impact on Irish society, if we exclude a cross, and memories and images most of which are somewhat faded and piecemeal now anyway. We know that the Pope couldn't go to the North because the Vatican had been persuaded that to do so would be unwise, on security grounds.

As for the spiritual shot in the arm that the visit was supposed to give to Irish Catholicism, that was also a vain hope. Forces were stirring in Irish society which even then militated against any renaissance. The slow but persistent spread of secularism, consumerism and materialism was already perceptible, if not measurable, in 1979.

Then there was the fact that the Irish Church itself was gripped by a kind of spiritual schizophrenia that ill-fitted it for the challenges that lay ahead. The rejection of the reforms of the Second Vatican Council (1962-65) and the as-yet-unseen influence of the papacy of Karol Wojtyla intensified that schizophrenia.

*

Among my memories of the 1979 visit, there are some that are comical and maybe even a bit farcical. Here's an example from the papal flight to Boston. Out over the Atlantic, a formidable figure in black emerged from the papal compartment on the Aer Lingus jumbo. The ex-footballer, who was now a Monsignor, took the cigar from his mouth and grunted: 'Guys, he ain't talkin'.'

The anxious journalists blinked in disbelief. What they were witnessing was like a scene from one of James Lee Burke's hard-boiled novels. Could this man, speaking the kind of dialogue more appropriate to a Sylvester Stallone movie, be the Pope's representative?

The prelate who had uttered the disappointing news was Paul Casimir Marcinkus. A towering hulk of a man who would go on to become an Archbishop and head of the Vatican Bank, he was widely known as 'the Pope's bodyguard'.

He certainly had the build and demeanour for the job: he looked and spoke like a Mafia don. Marcinkus, in his colourful way, had just told us that the Pope would not, as all of us hoped, be coming back to the plane to talk to the media. And there was no point in arguing – not with Marcinkus. He was six foot four and built like the Incredible Hulk. And he didn't stand on ceremony.

I first met him about four weeks before the Pope's visit. He had come over from Rome to check out the sites, the arrangements and the security for the papal trip. In Maynooth, where the Pope was to say Mass, Marcinkus asked to see the seating plan. When he saw a reference to nuns, he turned to Monsignor Michael Olden, who was then the president of Maynooth College, and instructed him as follows: 'No broads on the altar!'

That's Marcinkus for you. Now retired, he fell into disgrace after being at the centre of one of the greatest scandals in the history of the Catholic Church. That was when he moved on from being papal body-guard to papal banker. The sight of him with his cigar on the papal plane remains one of my enduring memories of 1979.

T. P. O'MAHONY is an author and journalist who has written for the *Examiner*, the *Kingdom* and the *Western People*, amongst other publications

'THE CLAPS AND CHEERS WOULD HAVE MADE
CROKE PARK ENVIOUS'

There was much talk – and many articles in the paper – about the coming of the Holy Father to Ireland. And on the twenty-ninth of September all our hopes were realised: John Paul II was really coming to our country. More exciting still, he was going to stay with the Papal Nuncio, Dr Alabrandi. The Nunciature is about three minutes away from the Dominican Convent.

As early as five o'clock on the morning of the twenty-ninth, hundreds of thousands of people walked through Phoenix Park, in prayerful silence, preparing for the unique occasion that was to come. At ten o'clock, the Aer Lingus jumbo *St Patrick* touched down at Dublin Airport; minutes later, John Paul II was on his knees kissing the Irish soil. The radio voice in the Phoenix Park called out 'He's here!': the claps and cheers from the crowd would have made Croke Park envious. That air of joyous happiness lasted the whole day as people made their way home after Mass.

The Pope's next call was Drogheda, but he remained on our side of the border. He told us all: 'Violence has no place in our lives. Stop the bombings and the shooting, and say your prayers more often.' If only they had listened to him and obeyed him.

On the Pope's return from Drogheda, he had group meetings with the Catholic bishops and the heads of other Churches, and a lively meeting with journalists and writers of all kinds in the convent.

At length he tried to return to the Nunciature, but a further crowd awaited him on the green opposite. Assisi House was in the process of being built, and they wanted him to bless the first stone. Meanwhile, they sang and entertained him. He wondered 'if the Irish ever go to bed.'

Next day, at 8 AM, it was the turn of the handicapped children of the area to meet the Pope. Many young people in wheelchairs came from Glenmaroon and St Vincent's on the Navan Road. Our own deaf children were there in great numbers with their attendants. We saw the tears in the Holy Father's eyes as he shook hands and blessed each one. It was like Our Lord's own days on earth.

Who can ever forget those days? His face, that smile, the infectious humour, the resonance of his voice, and the thunderous applause throughout the land. The way he kissed our stony ground and prayed. The way he held our children, placed his consecrated hands on their heads and told our young people: 'Children of Ireland, I love you.'

Truly, we in Ireland were blessed in every way through his coming in 1979.

SISTER CAMILLUS O'REILLY is a member of the Dominican Convent in Cabra, Dublin

189

CLONMACNOISE

In a quiet water'd land, a land of roses,
Stands Saint Kieran's city fair;
And the warriors of Erin in their famous generations
Slumber there.

There beneath the dewy hillside sleep the noblest
Of the clan of Conn,
Each below his stone with name in branching Ogham
And the sacred knot thereon.

There they laid to rest the seven Kings of Tara,
There the sons of Cairbrè sleep –
Battle-banners of the Gael that in Kieran's plain of crosses
Now their final hosting keep.

And in Clonmacnoise they laid the men of Teffia,
And right many a lord of Breagh;
Deep the sod above Clan Creidè and Clan Conaill,
Kind in hall and fierce in fray.

Many and many a son of Conn the Hundred-fighter
In the red earth lies at rest;
Many a blue eye of Clan Colman the turf covers,
Many a swan-white breast.

ANGUS O'GILLAN, translated from the Irish by T. W. ROLLESTON

'COULD I TOUCH THE POPE?'

Sunday 30 September 1979 saw a clear, bright dawn in Ireland. The day before, we had been glued to the television when Pope John Paul II arrived at Dublin Airport. That was a fine sunny day, with temperatures well above the average for the end of September. Everyone who watched him kiss the ground, as his cloak whirled about him, were captivated by the enormity of what was happening in our country. The subsequent visit to the Phoenix Park, the huge, tumultuous though reverential crowds, the Mass, the sermon, the blessing was a swirl of colour, commotion, joy and elation and we all marvelled at the rich tableau as it unfolded.

We lived in Athlone: my husband, Enda, and our two sons, Feargal, aged ten, and Aengus, fourteen. The Pope was coming to Clonmacnoise the next morning. He had expressed a wish to visit the ruins of one of the earliest sites of Christianity in Europe and one that had housed and tutored scholars from all over the continent. I was not in national public life at the time, although I was a member of both Athlone Town Council and Westmeath County Council: the invitation we received to go to Clonmacnoise had come through Enda's participation in the Midland Regional Tourism Organisation.

We were up at dawn: there was great excitement in the house as we ran around getting ready. Our hearts and minds were full of the wonderful spectacle of the Pope in the Phoenix Park the day before and what lay ahead of us in Clonmacnoise.

We set off around 6 AM: Clonmacnoise, although in County Offaly, is only about ten miles from Athlone. We joined the throng of cars and the very many people who were taking the Pilgrim Walk (as many had done of old) to the historic site. Clonmacnoise at that time, while many of its historic tombs and sites were preserved, was not in the wonderful state of preservation which it now is through the fine work of the Office of Public Works. We arrived, parked and walked for quite a distance, finally clambering on to the large site which slopes down to the River Shannon.

All around, people were climbing up on the headstones and jumping down. Then we heard the sound in the sky and the sight of the helicopter. Everyone rushed to where they thought the helicopter was going to land, and then of course were beaten back by the wind created by its blades. The Pope hopped out, robust and lively, as he then was, and kissed the ground of Clonmacnoise. I noticed how he looked around and took it all in – the Shannon and the people gathered there. You could see in his eyes and in his demeanour that he was genuinely happy to be there.

Clonmacnoise was an informal setting for the Pope. Even though there was a large Garda presence and he had his own security, he made it clear that he wanted to move about among the people, to meet them, talk to them, and pray with them, and so he did.

Aengus, my ten-year-old, was very struck by all that was happening. He plucked me and said: 'Could I touch the Pope?' 'Do, do, of course,' I replied, and he went over, pushed in and touched the Pope on the arm. I can see it yet: the Pope was reading one of the very old headstones and he turned around and blessed Aengus and put his hand on his head. It is one of my abiding memories: young Aengus, Pope John Paul II and that lovely, informal setting on that golden day.

As the Pope said in Rome on 17 October 1979: 'I wish in the first place to bear witness to the meeting with the mystery of the Church in the land of Ireland. I will never forget that place, in which we stopped for a short time, in the early morning hours, on Sunday 30 September: Clonmacnoise.'

MARY O'ROURKE is Leader of Seanad Éireann

'A DEFINING MOMENT IN IRISH HISTORY'

In my study there is a photograph which I have valued over the past twenty-five years. It captures a moment of conversation between Pope John Paul II, the Right Reverend Robert Heavener, Bishop of Clogher, and myself, then Bishop of Cork, Cloyne and Ross. This photograph was taken at a meeting of His Holiness with the Church of Ireland House of Bishops, the Honorary Secretaries of the General Synod of the Church of Ireland, and representatives of the other churches in the Dominican Convent in Cabra, Dublin.

Sometimes people enquire: what were you talking about? The Pope had asked where I ministered, to which I replied: 'Cork – the Passover City', explaining that the people of Cork regretted that, in the Pope's arduous pastoral tour, time had not permitted a visit to the second city of the Republic. Cork people, witty and proud, tried to conceal their disappointment by coining the phrase 'the Passover City'.

Our meeting was something of a disappointment. We had waited from 8 PM until 10.30 PM, when the exhausted Pope arrived after a gruelling day. He had given so much of himself to vast crowds, including his Drogheda message, with an unqualified condemnation of political violence in Ireland; there was time for only a few conversations and his brief address. In the circumstances, real dialogue was impossible.

Before the Pope's arrival in Ireland, the Archbishops of Armagh and Dublin had sent a letter of welcome to the Papal Nunciature. Also, there were sent gifts of a specially bound copy of *The Irish Book of Common Prayer* (1926) and a book by H. R. McAdoo, *The Spirit of Anglicanism* (1965). The letter expressed appreciation of the Pope's wish for peace and reconciliation, noting with concern the continuing problem of inter-church marriages in Ireland. Reference was made to the Anglican/Roman Catholic Commission on the Theology of Marriage (of which Archbishop George Simms was a member). It was hoped that a solution would be found to the stress and strain in this personal, family, community, and inter-church problem. I believe no reply was received to this letter.

The visit put the Churches of Ireland under the spotlight. The press, especially in the Republic, presented the Church of Ireland with a platform that was out of all proportion to our numerical size. The *Irish Times* carried an in-depth interview with the Bishop of Dublin in which Dr McAdoo spoke of the current ecumenical problems and opportunities. The *Irish Press* had an extensive article by Dr Arthur Butler, Bishop of Connor, entitled 'The Church of Rome through the Eyes of Protestants'. The *Press* also ran articles by Archbishop Simms of Armagh and Canon William Arlow of St Anne's Cathedral, Belfast, who was charged at that time with dealing with ecumenical and reconciliation issues. The *Furrow* featured an article by Dr R. H. A. Eames, Bishop of Derry and Raphoe.

Not all statements on the visit were uncritical. For example, the *Church of Ireland Gazette* carried an article by its columnist 'Cromlyn' entitled 'What I Would Like to Say to the Pope', which, with clarity and vigour, struck a chord with many members of the Church of Ireland, north and south.

In my presidential address to the Synod of the United Dioceses of Cork, Cloyne and Ross on 25 October 1979, I welcomed the visit, which would not be forgotten by large numbers of Roman Catholics and the wider Christian circle. I dared to declare that I found little in the Pope's addresses pointing to a pluralistic society for the Ireland of today. I went on to pose some questions, such as: 'Is it possible to be as certain of God's will about family planning in general and contraception in particular when, for example, one sees in the Third World death control without birth control?' 'Is the role of women to be as traditional as the Pope sees it?' 'Is there no possibility of change?'

Remember that these questions were raised in 1979: think of the changes that have occurred in both Church and society over the last quarter of a century – not all, but so many of them, for the good, especially in the field of inter-church relationships.

On the Sunday following this defining moment in Irish history, I was on a pastoral visit to a daughter church in the parish of Carrigaline in Cork. At the close of the service, outside, saying goodbye to the departing congregation, a little boy, possibly around eight or nine years of age, shook hands with me, saying: 'When is he going to make you a Cardinal?' There was no point in trying to get across to the child something of our unhappy divisions, so I replied: 'I'm afraid I will never be good enough to receive such a recognition.' As I drove back to Cork city, I pondered whether the little chap had seen the newspaper photograph that I mentioned above, or whether he had been prompted to pose the question by a naughty parent!

THE RIGHT REVEREND S. G. POYNTZ, Ph D, D Litt, was Bishop of Cork, Cloyne and Ross between 1978 and 1987, and Bishop of Connor from 1987 to 1995

'THE ONE PERSON WHO WOULD SEE IT WOULD BE GOD'

My name is written in blue paint on the topside of the Papal Cross in the Phoenix Park. Or at least, it was. The collapse of the church, and twenty-five years of vigorous sinning on my part, will have erased it by now. That, or the weather.

I wrote it myself, quickly and roughly – just my first name – using a small brush handed to me by a construction worker with a sense of theatre. The cross lay flat, ready to be raised. I was eye to eye with that part of it which would face the sky and which no one would ever see. There was a plate there, a couple of feet square – part of the welding arrangement, I suppose – where the man wrote the date and signed himself in, and then invited us kids to do the same. I was a little embarrassed. A timid thirteen-year-old with a very pubescent sense of the world, I wondered first whether it was allowed, and second, whether I could get away with writing something rude. But the man was keeping a solemn eye on us and all I could manage was a shaky approximation of my brand-new signature.

We lived just outside the Park gates, and the Park was, to a large extent, my world for much of my childhood. Most of the time, it seemed it was no one else's. Other people were a rare and usually resented presence. I didn't like it on weekends, or when it was very sunny. There were too many intruders around: noisy families, or inconveniently placed sun bathers, or people walking inappropriate dogs. But on weekdays, when I had finished or otherwise disposed of school, the place often felt like it was mine, and mine alone. And even if there were occasional dog walkers, they tended to be serious-minded people, walking serious dogs, and I approved of that. I patrolled, explored, usually on my bicycle, sometimes on foot, always off-road, discovering the paths and the tracks and the forests and the woods and the fields: the whole walled-in totality of it, like a flat planet.

I got to know its moods and its seasons and its deep and satisfying oddness. I had a map of it on my bedroom wall, with routes marked and landmarks circled; with links and associations, real and imagined and both, plotted and described and patterned; with annotations concerning not-fully-understood zones of possible danger or doubt or curious puzzlement. Such as the old well near the Furry Glen, where I had once seen a woman dip and bless herself backwards; or the Magic Wood, which, on certain days, was not there; or the Valley of Death, so named by my father, and where, I believed, so good is he at telling tales, that an actual battle had once taken place, with actual horses and actual men, who had been blown to ghostly pieces. I sometimes believed that I could hear them, thundering and crying and trampling the grass.

There were places where I would go carefully, with an intense, curious watchfulness. Such as the woods where my sisters had been flashed at; or the woods near the American ambassador's residence, where deer with massive antlers tended to linger, almost invisible in the clammy gloom. There was a lake beside which I often found the remains of small fires, and empty cans and bottles, and once, a rubber johnny. And then there were the broad rolling spaces where I could cycle or run or walk unnoticed by any human thing, and sink down into the long grass and look at the sky.

I don't remember what I thought of the idea of the Pope coming to disturb my peace. I probably thought it was great. I have always been a sucker for hype. I do remember, once the plans had been announced, cycling down to the inaccurately named Fifteen Acres to survey the proposed location. I couldn't understand how they were going to do it. No one would be able to see him. They'd have to put planks or something over the old water trough. The queue for Communion would take ages. I don't think there is any way at all that I could have conceived of the scale of it then.

Over the course of the weeks which led up to the end of September 1979, I began to get some idea of just how big it was going to be. The water trough disappeared. They put down a new road, a large area of tarmac, a helicopter pad. They built an artificial hill, and then covered it in steps and platforms, like the base of a pyramid. There was an endless line of trucks and lorries ferrying large pieces of equipment and infrastructure up and down the main park road. Bizarre pieces of shiny pliable scaffolding began to form erections of indeterminate purpose. Shirtless men with walkie-talkies and jeans and boots and muscles and helmets clambered over everything, manoeuvring cranes and rigging and decks and canvas.

I was very excited. It was like some kind of military encampment straight out of one of my comics. It was all male. It was bad language and English accents and sweat and grunting. And as long as I was home before dark and didn't get in anyone's way, it was mine to enjoy. Which I did, transfixed, and not quite understanding why.

It was something of a shock then when the cross arrived. Suddenly I was reminded of the point of it all. Pope. Mass. God. All that stuff. I hadn't seen a priest there the whole time. Even at home, the preparations had been entirely secular, with relatives I'd never heard of claiming sleeping-bag space on all of our floors, and my mother involved in a search for the lightest, sturdiest folding chairs in existence. In all the excitement, I had sort of forgotten about the Holy Father.

The cross lay flat on some kind of trailer. I thought it was ugly, but impressively heavy and big. I cycled a distance away from it when they raised it, partly because I wanted a better view, and partly because I was sure they'd drop it. It rose slowly, and awkwardly, with no grace at all, and as it came upright finally, and stood proud, all I could think about was how my name was written on the top of it, and how cool that was. And I thought too that no one would be able to see it, which was a pity, because invariably, no one would believe me that it was there at all. And I thought as well, finally, that the one person who would see it would be God. If he bothered to look down at the show, it would in fact be the first thing he'd see – my name, amongst some others, scrawled on the topside of a cross. A cross, he might have noticed, large enough to crucify a bigger God than him.

And the day itself? It was full of people. I remember the walk down there, in the first light. I remember us walking together, with our fold-up chairs under our arms, and our bags of sandwiches and our flasks. We walked through some of the places which I would have hesitated to venture into while on my patrols, and we were guided by ghostly men in armbands and their Sunday best, lurking behind trees. There were people everywhere. The park that I was used to seeing deserted was full. What was mine was everybody's. I didn't mind. I remember wondering whether I should mind – and I remember deciding that I didn't. I felt very generous. My world expanded and let everyone in.

Of the event itself, I can remember little. The best bit was when the Pope flew overhead in the jumbo. I worked out that he was at completely the wrong angle to see my name. Before he reappeared hours later – not nearly as impressively, in a helicopter – there was a long blur of excitement, anticipation and the terrible trips to the toilet. And all the time, a kind of breathless amazement at the size of the crowd – at the number of people it was possible to get into one place at one time. I kept on wandering off to see if I could see the edges. I couldn't. There was an ocean of laughter and babble that went on to the trees on all sides, as far as I could see and further. It moved me. In ways that only a timid thir-teen-year-old can be moved. I thought we were great. We were the best. People were amazing – and there were so many of them. I think my lit-tle heart fell in love that day with strangers. All strangers.

The Pope himself didn't seem to notice. I had thought he'd be as astonished as I was. But he gave no sign. I felt unable to say it, but it was like we'd thrown a surprise party and the guest of honour hadn't really noticed. The Mass was the most boring Mass I have ever attended. All the noise of humanity ceased, and the drone from the altar worked on the crowd like a soporific. It sounded distinctly out of place. I remem-ber feeling bad for yawning, but I couldn't stop myself. It was only after-wards, when he took to his mobile balcony and drove through the crowds, that we revived and began to enjoy ourselves again. There was a sense that it wasn't him showing himself to us that was exciting, but us showing ourselves to him. We took centre stage, and that was as it should be. We didn't want to steal the show, but we did, effortlessly.

Then he left.

We walked home, and looking back from the gates I saw the entire length of the main road alive with people, and the light looked beauti-ful, and the Phoenix Park was confirmed in my mind as the centre of the world.

What were we left with? For years and years afterwards, whenever my mother thought she might like to sit in the garden for a while, I was dispatched to the garage to get 'the Pope's chairs'. Ever since that time, whenever I am at an outdoor gig, and I see the roadies doing their thing before the band comes on, I think of the Pope. No one has ever believed me about my name being on the top of the cross. I have become an athe-ist and the type of person the Vatican refers to as 'objectively disor-dered' and 'evil.' (Congregation for the Doctrine of the Faith: 'Considerations Regarding Proposals to Give Legal Recognition to

Unions between Homosexual Persons'; the full text can be found at www.vatican.va.)

I am not, I think it's fair to say, well disposed towards the Pontiff. But nevertheless, I'm glad he came to the Park all those years ago, simply because so many people came to see him. It is a magical place. On that day it was fully human as well. It made me realise that God is what we become when we gather together. And that against that crowd, against the backdrop of just a million of us, a Pope like this one looks very grey, very small. Like a man who has missed the point.

Take down the cross.

KEITH RIDGWAY is the author, most recently, of the novel *The Parts*

'No dinners cooked and no cows milked

for the next three weeks'

My recollection of the Pope's visit to Knock in 1979 is one of great joy, enthusiasm and pride in our country. After all, the Pope was coming here; he wanted to visit us. There was a strange feeling in the air; everybody wanted to be part of the preparations.

My involvement in the papal visit started three weeks before the event, when members of the Apostolic Work Society were invited to Knock for a meeting with Archbishop Cunnane and Monsignor Horan. At that meeting, we were asked if we could make two hundred and fifty complete sets of vestments (each set consisting of an alb, a stole and a chasuble) for the clergy who would be celebrating Mass with the Pope. Nobody hesitated; there was unanimous agreement, although deep down we knew that the mammoth task facing us would mean no dinners cooked and no cows milked for the next three weeks.

There was a huge amount of behind-the-scenes activity, all very urgent, before we could start sewing. The design and trim of the vestments had to be approved by the authorities at Knock, the material and trim sourced, the design and instructions committed to paper, and copies to be sent with every parcel of material. As I happened to be in charge of the diocese (responsible for apostolic work) at the time and accommodation for apostolic work in the Parochial Centre was very small, the 'depot' became my home. The material was cut up there, parcelled and dispatched around the diocese. The design of the chasuble required a golden rose on the front: the children in Mrs McGovern's sewing class in St Joseph's Secondary School, Castlebar, stitched the two hundred and fifty golden roses required. The vestments were completed on time.

In the middle of this, another request came to us. The organisers of the event realized that they couldn't possibly supply enough regular ciboria for the distribution of Holy Communion. So they purchased a thousand wicker bread baskets – the types used for bread rolls at table – and asked the apostolic workers to line them with satin and make a lid which would be stitched on halfway round and hinged in the middle.

This arrangement would allow the priest to raise the lid sufficiently to get his hand in and, at the same time, protect the Hosts from the wind and rain. This we accomplished.

In appreciation of what Apostolic Work had contributed, I was selected as their representative to take part in the offertory procession. My gift was a stone from Croagh Patrick on a silver tray. The Pope touched the stone, and I handed it over to a priest. The priest then blessed me and shook my hand.

The only other person I knew in the offertory procession was Paul Connaughton from Mount Bellew. He was, or is, a Fine Gael TD. Another gift was St Jarlath's broken wheel, symbolizing the saint's founding of the diocese.

The Pope's vestments for Mass on his tours are sent ahead of him by the Vatican. Before he arrived in Knock, the sacristan, Sister Vincent, proceeded to lay out his vestments in readiness, only to discover that there was no alb. She remembered that Apostolic Work had left a few spares for emergencies, so she selected one and ironed it, and he wore it. We were chuffed that the Pope wore one of our albs. A few weeks later, the Apostolic Work Annual Diocesan Display was being held in Castlebar, and Father Fahey – a curate in Knock – arrived at the display with the alb and suggested that we display it with a tag saying it was the alb worn by the Pope at Mass in Knock. Word got out, and people started queuing to touch it: people who didn't get to Knock or, if they did, couldn't get near the Pope. I was terrified that the alb would get damaged, as it had to go back.

KATHLEEN RYAN was President of the Tuam Diocese, Apostolic Work, at the time of the Pope's visit to Ireland; she lives in Castlebar, County Mayo

'I BOUGHT A BANNER

AND MADE MYSELF A DUVET COVER FROM IT'

I was down the country when I got a call from Ronnie Tallon telling me that he had been asked to design the setting for the Papal Mass in the Phoenix Park, and would I join the team that he had assembled to deal with this very complex commission. He said it was like an open-air cathedral to hold a million people.

When I got to his office, he had already designed the great steel cross, standing on a stepped pyramid and backed by sixty banners, each sixty feet high. I was asked to design some giant banners, and got straight to work on them. I decided to use the papal coat of arms in the lower half and a strong yellow chevron pattern on the top, which helped to form a link between all the banners.

The design was approved by the Hierarchy, and I immediately flew to Manchester to find cotton of the right strength and size. I then located a silk-screen printer that was big enough to print them. Several convents had been asked to handle the sewing of the banners, so I could relax!

Two days before the Mass, we started hanging some of the banners. There was a fresh wind from the west, and it was noticed that some of the sewing was beginning to pull apart. We quickly identified which bundle the faulty banners came from. The convent was phoned; needless to say, they were distressed, and they told us to bring them back. By this time, I had arrived on the scene, and realised we had to act fast. I said to put the faulty bundle in my car and give me a police escort. So off I went with two Garda outriders. I duly delivered the banners to the distressed nuns, who had them repaired and back to the Park the next morning.

On the day itself, I drove early to the Park and got myself to the allotted corral. The banners were all in place, but the wind shifted to the east and was gusty. I was afraid that the change in wind direction would blow the top arm around and expose the back of the banners. But that only happened to one of them.

I bought a banner from the auction later and made myself a duvet cover from it. Now I sleep well under the papal arms and don't have nightmares about the wind changing.

PATRICK SCOTT is an artist living in Dublin; he designed the banners and signs for the Phoenix Park Mass

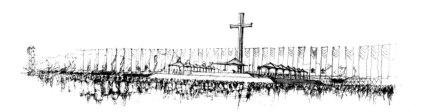

213

'THE EXALTATION OF THE CROSS'

At the beginning of August 1979, I received a call from the Archbishop of Dublin appointing our practice to design and builf an outdoor event for the celebration of Mass for one million people. He had just received confirmation that the Pope was coming to Ireland in eight weeks' time. His confidence in our ability to design and coordinate the physical requirements on the day was terrifying. No one had experience of planning the assembly of people on that scale, and on a site in the Phoenix Park that had no services available. Cardinal Hume had advised Rome that such an event could not be structured in eight weeks. The challenge was set.

Working closely with my partners, Robin Walker, Niall Scott, Joan Tallon and Stephen Woulfe Flanagan, over the weekend, a design strategy was agreed. George Sisk and Co. were appointed managing contractors, and all building workers were recalled from holidays. With the approval of Monsignor Tom Fehily, the executive director, the task commenced. So many tasks, so many experts collaborating. Public and private sectors working closely together with amazing respect and trust. I will look at one task only: the making and erection of the cross, to illustrate the efforts that were put into staging the event.

We decided that we required a cross the height of Nelson's Pillar, which was 125 feet high, which would be clearly visible to all from the furthest reaches of the vast congregation and which would give a sense of focus to the occasion. The cross would need to be raised on a podium approximately one acre in area, lifting the Papal Altar to a height that would allow sightlines from the far corner of the two-hundred-acre site and allow everyone a view of the ceremony.

A check was made with the international steel mills to establish what sections of steel they were rolling in that week. The rolling schedule for one section of steel could be extended if we confirmed the order within twenty-four hours. The steel section that was proposed was 750 cm by 150 cm; it would require six of these rollings welded together to provide a section capable of rising 125 feet high. Thirty tons of this steel section and forty miles of welding would be required to construct it.

215

Frantic phone calls to the Archbishop's house requesting that they approve the ordering of the material within twenty-four hours, or we could not produce the cross, met with an immediate act of faith. The steel mills rolled the entire thirty tons of section over a weekend and delivered it to Dublin the following week.

J&C McGloughlin, great steel fabricators of that period, undertook the task of fabricating the cross to our design. Ove Arup and Partners, the structural engineers, checked the design for dynamic gust analysis and cross-wind oscillations. Welders came out of retirement to join the team, which produced forty miles of intricate welding in four weeks. To give some idea of the enthusiasm of the people involved in the project, we had hundreds of phone calls from craftsmen in Dublin, anxious to contribute and offering their services free. Everyone wanted to play a part in making this historic gathering a success.

To support the cross, a great reinforced concrete box was constructed on-site during the four weeks required for welding off-site. This structure formed the centre of the altar podium and the structural support for the cross. It supported the altar and altar canopy; the robing chamber and rest area for the Pope were accommodated within the concrete box. The concrete structure also served as the anchor for the one-acre podium constructed with scaffolding and boarding. The entire podium was covered in a carpet that was specially designed to give the appearance of granite.

The cross was brought to the Phoenix Park in sections and welded in its final form on the ground. Two weeks before the great day, on the fourteenth of September, the cross was lifted into position using two hundred-ton cranes. The cross was then bolted down to its base and secured. John Donat, in an article on the design strategy, has recorded that: 'By a happy coincidence, completely unplanned, this day happened to be the Church's Feast of the Exaltation of the Cross.'

The cross remains today as a reminder of a perfect moment when more than one and a quarter million people assembled to celebrate the first visit of a Pope to our shores.

RONNIE TALLON, an architect and co-founder of Scott Tallon Walker Architects, designed the Papal Cross

216

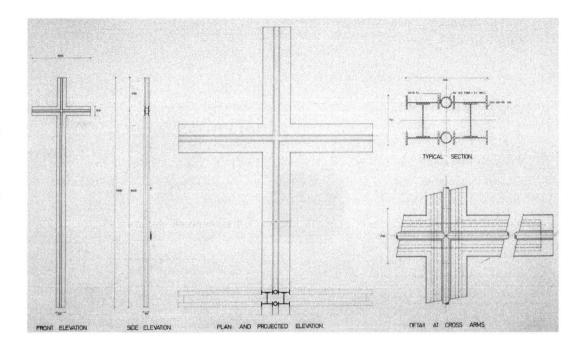

FRONT ELEVATION.   SIDE ELEVATION.   PLAN AND PROJECTED ELEVATION.   DETAIL AT CROSS ARMS.

TYPICAL SECTION.

'THERE WAS AN INSTANT RESPONSE TO HIS WORDS'

I am regularly amazed by, and sometimes a little envious of, people who have the capacity to recall details of events long passed. I have no such gift. When, therefore, I was asked to write something of my memories of the Pope's visit to Ireland in 1979 – yes, I had to look up the exact year – my immediate inclination was to plead amnesia, but I'm not good at saying 'no'.

Yes, I do remember some things: the sheer excitement of seeing on television the papal jet appear in the skies above Dublin Airport, the sense of togetherness of people during the days of his visit, the joy of the Galway celebration, the sadness that his passionate plea for an end to violence in Northern Ireland evoked little response.

I attended the Galway celebration. Even the journey from Ennis in the early hours of the morning was special: there was an empathy with fellow travellers, who seemed more friendly and considerate then usual. I was still teaching at second level at the time and joined a large group of students from the school at the Galway Racecourse. Bishop Eamonn Casey and Father Michael Cleary played prominent roles in setting the atmosphere for the arrival of the Holy Father. There was a wonderful spirit of palpable friendship among the people.

I remember little of the ceremony apart from the long snake-like procession of white-robed clergy making their way from a distant factory premises across the racecourse towards the altar. I still recall, however, something of the homily directed specially to young people: the appeal to them not to be taken in by the prospect of immediate gratification offered to them in today's world.

Is there anyone who does not remember the Pope's 'Young people of Ireland, I love you'? Perhaps overuse of the quote has dulled its meaning, but I still remember its powerful impact on all of us – and I wasn't young at the time! In hindsight, it seemed such a simple thing to say, but somehow no one had said it before – certainly not with that degree of conviction, which made it clear to all of us who were listening that he did truly love and care about the young people of Ireland. There was an instant response to his words, a tangible expression of joy leading to

219

'He's got the whole world in his hands', sung in unison across the race-course.

It is all too easy to say: 'God loves us' or 'We must love our neighbour'. The phrases are vague and unchallenging. It takes courage to say: 'I love you.' That is real; it is personal. I happen to believe that the very statement 'Young people of Ireland, I love you' gave many of us a bit more freedom and courage to admit to and give public expression to our own deeper emotions than we had heretofore. Could Joe Connolly have used the phrase to the people of Galway in receiving the McCarthy Cup in 1980 if the Pope hadn't used it the previous year?

I attended the Limerick ceremony too but have little memory of it. Perhaps it is because I cheated in getting there. Most people had journeyed through the darkness of night and were waiting for hours at the Limerick venue. I journeyed at the last minute, when the roads were empty. I got there without any hardship and remember little from it. No pain, no gain? I simply recall that the Holy Father spoke on the family.

Those were days of innocence, still some years away from the harsh realities which have since caused us so much pain. Yes indeed, but still I am grateful to have been part of it all.

BISHOP WILLIE WALSH is the Bishop of Killaloe, which includes parts of Clare, Laois, Offaly, Limerick and Tipperary

THE POPE IN GALWAY

When grey dawn broke on misty morn
O'er Galway's racecourse wide,
Then youth emerged from sleeping bags
Like newborn butterflies.

Their vigil kept throughout the night,
In bag or bus or car,
They came from homes throughout the land,
The youth from near and far.

Then screaming through the morning air
Came helicopters loud,
And Pope John Paul was standing there,
Hands raised in blessing crowd.

His words came in compassion wrapped,
In loving phrases bound,
And in those words, inspired and true,
Was deep faith to be found.

He gave them guides by which to live,
In most harmonious way,
He told the youth that he loved them
And trusted them that day.

And Godly vibes with saintly hue
Went flowing o'er the crowd;
With wild, restrained effusion,
They sang heart-deep and loud.

Famed bishops and great singing priests
Seemed merely atoms then,
For God had sent his vicar here
To stir the hearts of men.

And though it be a thousand years
Before he comes again,
His loving words and smiling tears
Will guard our faith till then.

PAT WATSON of Bealnamulla, County Roscommon, was a steward in
Galway for the Youth Mass

225

'COULD YOU ARRANGE FOR ME TO MEET THE POPE?'

I was twelve years of age when John F. Kennedy visited Ireland in June 1963. I remember that there was great excitement in our house and around the neighbourhood. All the talk on the radio was about this Irish-American president coming home. I knew it was a big event but perhaps did not fully realise what it meant to those who were older than me and more familiar with the great man.

Sixteen years later, I was a member of Dublin Corporation, which was in overdrive following the announcement that His Holiness Pope John Paul II was to visit Ireland. Now this was big: the first ever visit of a Pope to Ireland. The country was awash with excitement at the thought that the Pope would be celebrating Mass with us on our own soil, speaking to us in our homeland. Could we cope with such a visit? Were we prepared for the logistical challenges involved. Would the venues be ready on time? Of course we could handle such an enormous undertaking. The Pope was visiting Ireland: we had to!

Meetings followed meetings. I remember a colleague asking me one evening as we went into the Corporation offices what sort of numbers did I think would attend the open-air Mass in the Phoenix Park. 'A million, maybe,' I mused. Later, I thought: hold on, a third of the population of the country in the Park on one day? Maybe not.

I remember people coming into my weekly clinics just to ask me about the visit, and where they could get the best view of His Holiness? One lady asked me if I could arrange for her to meet him. People sometimes attribute too much power to us politicians!

We all knew and expected that, as he did everywhere he visited, the Pope would kneel and kiss the ground – a truly unique gesture he had developed. Shivers ran up my spine when he did so on the tarmac of Dublin Airport. I know that is a hackneyed term, but it is about the only way I know to describe the effect it had on me and on countless others at the time.

For me, the lead-up to the open-air Mass in the Phoenix Park was memorable. I still find it hard to give a good pen picture to my daughters of what it was like to see hundreds of thousands of people moving towards the Phoenix Park in the small hours of the morning. I remem-

227

ber families from my own constituency, small children in their parents' arms, heading for the Park. Some people were walking along singing hymns, and others were even reciting the rosary. People were tucking into sandwiches which were probably to last them the rest of the day, and groups of people were sipping cups of tea under lampposts at the side of the road. I saw a queue of at least thirty people at a public phone in Amiens Street – this was in the days before mobile phones – probably telling folks in the country that they had arrived safely.

And then came the realisation that, although everyone knew that huge numbers were expected for the Mass, there were a million of us there. A million! At times when I pass through the Phoenix Park, the thought strikes me: how did we all fit in?

My reflections on the visit a quarter of a century later are that it had a profound effect on people in Ireland at the time. His Holiness was early in his pontificate; we knew of his experiences in Poland during the war; he was venturing out of the Vatican with a regularity that was previously unheard of; he was visiting a country that professed itself in the main to be part of his flock; and it was the first ever visit by a Pope to these shores. Those who experienced the visit of Pope John Paul II were left with memories that will last a lifetime.

An Taoiseach Bertie Ahern td

229

231

233